# *Fishing* ── IN THE ── FOOTSTEPS OF # MR. CRABTREE

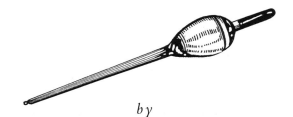

*by*

## JOHN BAILEY

WITH ILLUSTRATIONS BY

## ROBERT OLSEN

FOR BOB AND MIKE HOLCOMBE
AND SARAH.

First published in Great Britain by Mr. Crabtree Publishing, 2012.

Words © John Bailey, 2012
Illustrations © Robert Olsen, 2012.

Author: John Bailey

Illustrations, cartoon story lines, design and typography: Robert Olsen

Executive Editor: Paula Battle

Consulting Editor: Lester Holcombe

Associate Editors: Andy Anderson and James Arnold–Baker

Contributors: Hannah Bruford, Hugh Miles, Chris Yates, Pat O'Reilly,
Terry Hearn, Kevin Nash, Kevin Clifford, Ali Hamidi and Keith Arthur.

Original Bernard Venables illustrations from Mr. Crabtree Goes Fishing © Mirror Group Newspapers.

Printed and produced exclusively in the U.K. by Butler, Tanner and Dennis.

Published by Mr. Crabtree Publishing under licence from Mirror Group Newspapers.

ISBN 978 0 9573992 0 4

Typeset in 11.5/16.75pt Bembo.

Mr.Crabtree
PUBLISHING

# Contents

*Hannah Bruford, daughter of Bernard Venables, with her brothers Aaron and Guy.*

# Foreword

## Hannah Bruford

Our childhood was steeped in fishing, Mr. Crabtree, and all the other projects that Dad was involved in.

One of my earliest memories is of an enormous fish, which I understood to be a shark, laying the full length along the floor of our larder.

We were surrounded by fishing equipment. We grew up in a large, rambling farmhouse that sat on top of a hill, the nearest road a mile away. The attics of the house were a place of curiosity, wonder and play. They were dusty storerooms; in places slits of sunlight would appear through the plaster and brick.

There were suitcases with tags and labels that spoke of exotic and exciting places, Zambia, Tanzania and The Azores. Names of places that had amazing tales attached, such as witches in Africa, thundering hippopotami and Dad being imprisoned for taking photos. There were chests of drawers filled with reels, lines, hooks and floats. The most exciting – far too big to fit in a drawer - was the enormous shiny metal reel that was wound with wire cable for line and the equally large stout leather harness that Dad had used to catch the big shark.

We helped him prepare bait by putting stale bread and water into big metal bins. We were taught to cast a fly line from an early age using a devilish arrangement of a rod barely four feet long that had a broad, fluffy, bright pink wool line attached. Dad always said that if we could cast with that, we could cast with anything.

I remember my fascination with the routine of cartoon strips, such as Crabtree, being created. Dad would pencil sketch in the boxes and text bubbles. They would then be posted, only to re-appear later with the text magically inked in. Dad would then draw in the images with a brush and ink.

It was a childhood of contradictions, having little in terms of material possessions but rich in exposure to art, music and the natural world. Living in a run-down farmhouse and yet hearing talk of grand people such as Charles of the Ritz.

I remember the preparations for exhibitions. Pictures being finished, aware of the frustration in waiting for the oils to dry before the last touches could be added, framing completed, then going with Dad to attend the exhibition. Our childish excitement if a red sold dot appeared on one of the pictures.

Discussions took place around the dinner table about the future of the planet, from self-sufficiency to preserving waterways, globalisation to the perils of not eating a healthy diet. We were encouraged to think and to wonder at the natural world around us. We would wander for hours through the woods and fields. One day I found a weasel caught in a trap. I ran the two miles home to get Dad. He stopped what he was doing and came back with me and freed the little wild animal.

That made him a hero in my eyes.

# Mr. Crabtree Goes Fishing

## Hugh Miles

There appears to be a time in an angler's life when where, how and when you fish becomes much more important than what you catch and I'm grateful that I, for one, have reached that happy stage. Close friends and others of a similar generation call these magic combinations 'pure Crabtree' and it is thanks to Bernard that these moments are still as wonderful in real life as when he first created them.

I was fortunate to grow up with Bernard's creation as my bible and, as all those who have read it know, the book is full of wisdom and good sense. But even more important than that, it inspires a love of wild places and the fish that live there through the seasons.

How can you not be inspired by the shoal of perch chasing minnows, the pike sweeping aggressively after the spinner, the roach in the Avon and local canal, the tench bubbles or perhaps best of all, the shoals of glorious rudd in the Norfolk Broads. As a boy, I just had to share all these experiences, try to turn dream into reality… and to this day I still do, the images indelibly etched into my memory.

Fishing with my childhood hero was as inspiring as his fictional character, for Bernard's tireless enthusiasm was as infectious as Mr. Crabtree's was to Peter. On one memorable days barbel fishing with him on the River Kennet, he knelt by a promising swim for several hours, holding his rod and feeling for bites… and that was when he was approaching his ninetieth birthday. No chairs or bolt rigs for this sensitive, creative, gentle man.

Given his character, his knowledge and creative talents, it is no surprise that the legacy of his writing and art will live on in our hearts and minds forever. Much has changed in the natural world since he created Crabtree, but we might do well to remember to show our new generations of anglers the angling principles he introduced us to. As us old anglers say, it's not how to catch but how to enjoy.

# Saint Bernard

## Chris Yates

I only knew Bernard for the last 13 years of his life, but in that time he became a good friend and now that he's fishing in that great pond in the sky, no doubt with Izaak Walton, I miss him very much.

What always impressed me about him was his genuine love for all those things that made life worth living, like trees, beer, books, art, untramelled landscapes, rivers, lakes and, of course, fish. Bernard could enthuse about almost any species of fish as if each one was the most magical creature on Earth and he had just discovered it. I remember him singing the praises of the tench during one of our first meetings, glorying in its beautiful colour and form and wishing he knew the whereabouts of some lilied pond like the one he used to fish in his youth. I said there was such a place not far from my cottage and so, naturally, we arranged a day's tench fishing.

The pond we visited was less than an acre, fringed with reeds, edged by lilies, overhung by willows. It contained, said Bernard, after we had a quiet saunter around the banks, a distillation of all the best tench fishing qualities.

Such was his appreciation of the water and his eagerness to cast his float that he began to remind me not of the great Crabtree but the gleeful excitable son, Peter. We were soon happily watching our painted quills as they sat next to the lily pads, and though several hours passed with only a couple of small fish coming to my rod Bernard's optimism was unshakable. It was, therefore, a great delight to us both when his amber-coloured float began to drift, tremble and then lie flat in an almost perfect reprise of the tench fishing sequence in Mr. Crabtree. After the strike, Bernard's rod curved towards a stubborn, tough-fighting fish, but I got the net under it in the end and we celebrated the capture of a typical pond tench: a lovely green-glowing three-pounder.

Nowadays, whenever I leaf through the pages of Crabtree, I like to pause at the tench fishing chapter, because it always evokes more than just the quiet magic of that kind of fishing; it brings back the book's creator as well and reminds me of that day at the pond. And, anyway, it was one of the favourite chapters of my boyhood, back in the early Sixties, when I used to read and reread the book and dream about catching a tench myself.

# Bernard's Inspiration

### Kevin Clifford

We are all creatures of our time and the influence of Bernard Venables and his Mr. Crabtree Goes Fishing is essentially confined to people of my age group – the baby boomers born after the Second World War. Those impressionable youngsters were captivated in what was still a naive world by the weekly episodes of Mr. Crabtree and Peter. Yes, it was all a bit unrealistic, but that didn't matter a single jot. The objective worked, Mr. Crabtree got youngsters hooked on fishing and made them want to get out onto the banks.

I only met Bernard Venables once, and what little I know of the man suggests our characters are poles apart. But I owe him a huge debt for that early influence of Mr. Crabtree, for it was to put me on a path where angling infects almost every aspect of my being. Undoubtedly, Mr. Crabtree did the same for so many of my age group and Bernard's inspiration is somehow, almost magically, passed along in the very DNA of angling.

# Crabtree & Me

### Pat O'Reilly

1947... my first fish on rod and line. Beautiful. Many 'learning experiences' followed that early success. From zero knowledge how could a youngster learn? Answer: with pages torn from the Daily Mirror. I went fishing with a striding, pipe-smoking expert. Roach, pike, trout, bass – we caught plenty, and gradually I learned why. Without Mr. Crabtree I would have become a very different kind of fisherman, maybe even an ex-fisherman.

Fast forward (much too fast) half a century: I was still learning from the creator of my virtual tutor, now a close friend. Bernard Venables and I would lunch together and then try for trout on his beloved Avon, or for salmon on my adopted river, the Teifi, where Bernard had cast while Mr. Crabtree Goes Fishing was my bedtime reading.

At 90 Bernard could not walk across the meadow to the riverbank: his enthusiasm still drove him to run. With fading sight that was risky, so I ran too. We talked of the nature of fish, of rivers, of trees, of life. I listened mostly and came to appreciate how great Bernard Venables was; how lucky I and countless other young Peters were that Mr. Crabtree communicated his passion so infectiously.

# Crabtree Infusions

### Ali Hamidi

It's really strange that even though I had never read any of Mr. Crabtree's material, or even looked at it, that name became impregnated in my head very early on in my fishing life!

I suppose that is testimony to the impact that the Crabtree name had on so many people throughout angling. It was so strong that eventually they would pass it onto future generations of anglers, without them actually really ever reading any of the material first hand.

When I think of Mr. Crabtree, I think of a lovely flowing river, with a narrow overgrown path leading to a sloped brambled gap, uncomfortable to fish, but clearly home to many specimens! It was in a swim very similar to this that I quoted the name "Mr. Crabtree" on TV whilst filming Thinking Tackle. Did I really know for sure, that this "swim is very Mr. Crabtree"?

Does it really matter?

Mr. Crabtree had somehow got into my head.

# 3 Generations of Crabtree Influence

## Terry Hearn

I think I was a bit too young, or possibly not even born when the Mr. Crabtree strips were running in the Daily Mirror. I'm embarrassed to say that I don't remember reading the books either, but I still think that Bernard Venables' work had a great influence on my own fishing.

As a kid my grandad used to take me fishing lots. I'd regularly stop over at his house the night before and he'd tell me so many fishing stories, and get me so excited that I'd struggle to get off to sleep. Summer stories of wily tench and crucian carp bubbling alongside a float, and autumn tales of monster barbel, powerful fish that were nearly always lost. When one was finally banked it would have several hooks in its mouth from all the anglers that had lost an epic battle with it in the past. "No way!" I'd say, surely I'd never manage to land such a strong fish myself...

I'd dream about fishing all night long and then, once grandad had woken me in the early hours of the morning, the fishing stories would carry on as he made the flasks and pork dripping sandwiches for the day. There were the tales of eels so big that he'd hang them up on the door at home (grandad always ate them...) and their tails would almost reach the floor! Monster pike, huge perch, no matter what the species, my grandad had a story for them.

Knowing what I know now, and having since seen many a republished Mr. Crabtree strip, I think the great man himself had heavily influenced my old grandad. So many of his stories were along the same lines. Things like tench bubbling alongside a float and carp circling a piece of floating crust several times before eventually taking it. I may not have been a reader of the Daily Mirror myself, but I think my grandad certainly was! Maybe some of his stories were embellished a little, but it matters not for he played a huge part in firing up the angler inside of me.

The greatest inspirations of our time go on inspiring forever, and sometimes their inspiration rubs off on so many people that the true source of that inspiration can easily be forgotten. With all that he wrote and all that he did, Mr. Crabtree was clearly a giant of a man, and no matter how young or old the angler in you may be, I think that we've all been influenced by his character. For certain my grandfather was influenced by him, as was my own father, and though I missed out on the original series of strips in the Daily Mirror, so was I.

# The Birth of an Angler

Kevin Nash

There was a swirl, and then the duckweed parted as it danced and shimmered in the vortex. The boy dipped his net and lifted. He struggled; it was so heavy – much heavier than it should have been for the capture of a tadpole or a newt. He gasped when he saw the fish – and what a fish! Thick-set, deep and armoured with the most golden of scales, its huge mouth opened and closed and its dorsal fin bristled. The boy looked on in wonder. He had never seen such a beautiful fish and wondered what it could be.

On Monday, after school, the boy visited the village library. He was still thinking about the magnificent golden fish. In fact, that was all he thought about while at school that day. His lessons had been in vain; his teachers' words never heard.

He browsed the library shelves, wondering where to look. Then he saw a book, 'Mr. Crabtree Goes Fishing'. He reached up for it, stretching his body from the tips of his toes, barely managing to lift the large book off the shelf. He liked this book because it had realistic drawings, just like his favourite comic.

As he thumbed through the pages he stopped suddenly. There was a picture of Mr. Crabtree's son, Peter, with a fish – it was the boy's fish. He read the words and discovered that it was a carp.

He took the book to the library table and commenced reading, his anticipation and excitement growing as every page was turned. He wanted to be Peter and have a dad like Mr. Crabtree. He glanced at the clock. He was very late and would have to run all the way home, or face a beating.

It was the evening of the 8th July, 1963. The time was ten to six. At that moment a lifelong fisherman was born. That boy was me.

# Lessons of Crabtree

## Keith Arthur

I was just turning into a teenager when Mr. Crabtree Goes Fishing was published and, naturally, I was one of the millions that bought it. Fishing was more simple then – not as good as today in many instances, but certainly more simple. I learned from the book that if I wanted to catch a big chub, I needed to go to The Royalty but within a couple of years I'd managed some smaller chub – on Mr. Crabtree tactics of course – from the lovely flowing stretches of my more local River Lea. What's more I caught them trotting with a bodied quill float, from an identical swim to the one Mr. Crabtree described.

When my angling career developed I took what for many would be considered the 'left-hand-path' of match angling and, eventually, became quite proficient but I always remembered the sort of swim Mr. Crabtree showed Peter and I suppose his key unlocked the door to the magic kingdom of watercraft, the inherent knowledge of knowing where fish should be. And when I can't catch them I will always put that down to my own inadequacies rather than a mistake on Crabtree's part.

To this day, when fishing with friends, I will often describe a particularly evocative stretch of water as in "a real Crabtree swim" and although I never managed to catch that big Royalty chub, one of the greatest thrills of my earlier angling days, on my very first visit to that hallowed stretch of the Hampshire Avon, I actually carried a fish to the very same weighing room and, on a slightly different set of scales, with a weight pan rather than a dial, laid a barbel that another idol, the late Jack Harrigan, assured me was a barbel well over the minimum 10lbs required to be weighed therein. It weighed 9lb 11oz 12dr and I've felt a fraud ever since.

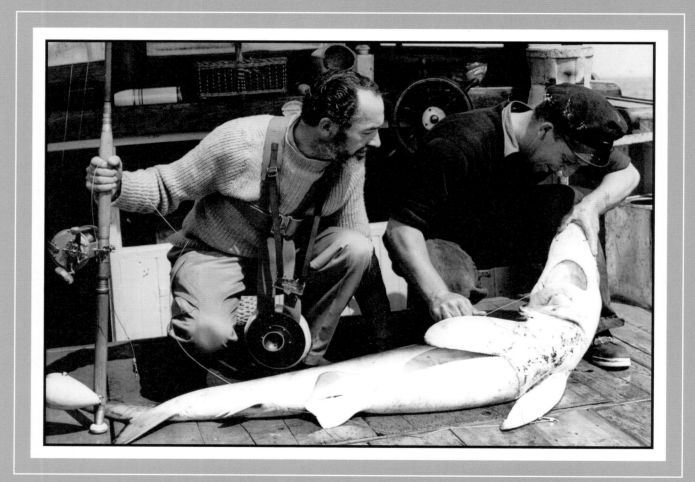

# Mr. Crabtree Introduction

We all have a Crabtree story and out of the shoals of mine I will start with one that shows just how real and how beloved a cartoon character can be. Imagine the scene, not very long ago, down on the River Wye, a bankside tea party of anglers turned Crabtree. The Kelly Kettle was in full steam, the cake was being cut and Mr. Crabtree became the focus of our attention though, as one of the group said, he's never far away from it.

Who taught Mr. Crabtree to fish was the first conjecture? He was obviously part of a caring family and society we guessed. Possibly his own father, uncle or perhaps an older brother took young Master Crabtree to the riverbank for the first time. Mr. Crabtree was obviously good at relationships. Think how easy and informal his manner is with Peter and how he imbues every fishing trip with information and enthusiasm.

More frivolously, we wondered what Mr. Crabtree's Christian name might be. Something traditional surely? Henry, Edward, Wilfred, Thomas or Richard were the proffered possibilities. My suggestion of Basil won on a narrow vote. How about his age? We guessed that he probably just missed the Great War and, if Peter were around 10, that might put Mr. Crabtree in his mid-40s when they set out together. Men like Mr. Crabtree tended to wait until they were financially established before beginning a family.

What about his occupation? There is no sign of a car to suggest extreme affluence, but that would not be unusual so soon after the war outside of the so-called very upper classes. One wag suggested he may have been a tobacconist! An accountant found some favour amongst the group but in the end, we decided to plump for bank manager. Mr. Crabtree obviously was not without money. All of his and Peter's fishing tackle was well up to the mark and they could obviously afford to visit places like the Royalty, presumably by train. There is also the mysterious Patsy to whom Mr. Crabtree and Peter took home the odd perch or two. One would presume Patsy was a cook or a maid, perhaps, who helped Mrs. Crabtree keep the home fires burning. Nonsense as this story might seem, I've chosen it to serve a purpose. The fact that six anglers aged between 21 and 67 can spend a fascinating hour discussing such things does show how central the cartoon character called Mr. Crabtree can be. Herein lies my nervousness.

There's a potential problem about commenting on a book if you've been exceptionally close to it for the vast majority of your life. This is how I have been with the legendary Bernard Venables' work, Mr. Crabtree Goes Fishing. Its role so dominated my early years that it is perhaps difficult for me now to describe its merits dispassionately. Over the last year, largely because we have been filming Fishing in the Footsteps

of Mr. Crabtree, I have gone back to the book with the same ferocious enthusiasm that I had for it as a child. I can see that my adoration was not displaced. Mr. Crabtree Goes Fishing truly is a legendary piece of work. It deserves its hallowed place in angling literature. I think now it is possible to admire it both from a child's point of view and as a grown-up.

As a child, I found Mr. Crabtree wholly inspirational. We all did. Initially, it was all about the immediacy of Bernard's cartoons. There is no doubt they shaped my angling ambitions almost entirely. They also led me into a fantastic fishing world of adventure that seemed so real I felt I could almost touch it, almost be a part of it. There's a cliché in fishing that we all fell asleep with Mr. Crabtree on our pillows and this is not fabrication. It's an important moment in a tired child's life when he falls asleep, his thoughts centred on the things that mean most to him. Mr. Crabtree figured in endless dreams for millions of us.

Mr. Crabtree signposted my future. Those cartoons fired ambitions that I have realised one by one throughout my lifetime. When I first read Mr. Crabtree, I had no opportunity and certainly not the talent nor the skill to catch barbel, carp, tench, pike or big roach. As the years have progressed and my abilities have grown, there have been many moments when it has seemed that I have been living out the scenes that I used

to dream about fifty years ago. When I first read Mr. Crabtree I was fishing the canals of the northwest and a roach of a few ounces was truly a whopper. The thought of landing a roach in a swollen winter river and casually estimating it at a pound and a half, like Mr. Crabtree did, was way beyond my ken. When at last I began to catch two-pound roach with regularity, I felt sometimes as though I were fishing in a cartoon myself. When I began to catch the fish that Mr. Crabtree had led me to dream about, it was as though my life had finally found the purpose that I'd always wanted from it.

It wasn't just fish that Mr. Crabtree made me, made all of us, aspire to catch. Mr. Crabtree hooked us on the waters that the fish lived in. Like Peter, I yearned to fish the beautiful rivers and lakes of this country and, eventually, of the world itself. Through the cartoons, I watched Mr. Crabtree and Peter either walk or cycle to places that, as a child, I could only dream of. It was important to me that when I moved to Norfolk as a youngster, these wonderful, enchanting paradises, one by one, seemed to open up to me. I still have not lost that child-like wonder that I always feel when I stumble across a new water that is close to perfection.

Of course, more down to earth, Mr. Crabtree was vital to me, and to all of us children, because he passed on information. Mr. Crabtree taught us how to fish with extreme simplicity and total direction. Mr. Crabtree didn't do fuss or over-complication. The tackle, the rigs, the presentation and the bait were all described in such a way that made them easy to grasp and to understand. Mr. Crabtree spouted no jargon and no gobbledegook. There was nothing that Mr. Crabtree taught Peter that, even as a six year old, I couldn't get my head around.

I remember a little old brick pit in Greater Manchester where my friends and I used to gather in school holidays. The rumour was that it was bottomless and, if we had enough line, our baited hook would eventually catch a fish down in Australia. That was the legend of Sammy's Pit for you, but what I do remember for sure is that one day, in bright sunlight, my mates and I saw a small tench in the margins and we all but swooned with excitement. We had a real Mr. Crabtree pow-wow. It was like he was there looking out for us. A couple of us began to dig up lobworms. Another lad cycled off to the bakers with a few pence that we'd managed to rustle up between us. We tried with floats and then ledgers and finally caught the tench on half a lobworm after it had refused bread flake. I've never seen a tench caught more simply and it was all down to the lessons of Mr. Crabtree.

One thing Mr. Crabtree gave me as a child was confidence. I never picked up Crabtree and felt in any way belittled or overawed. Mr. Crabtree made us believe that fishing is for all

of us, not just for the experts. This is exactly what I believe today. It's how I actually regard my own fishing abilities. I don't think I'm much better at the sport than I was when I was a teenager. My methods haven't advanced much even though I've got better tackle and baits at my disposal. All I've really done is build up my knowledge of watercraft and fish behaviour and that's about it. I had enough confidence to catch fish years ago and that self-belief passed on by Mr. Crabtree has sufficed all my angling life.

As children, Mr. Crabtree helped us with our relationships. Having a mentor is vital in the lives of the young when it comes to fishing, or indeed any aspect of life. To this day, I harbour a lurking regret that I never once fished with my father but there were plenty of northern working men who did fish and were happy to take me with them in vans, in three-wheelers and in charabancs to places way beyond my pedal power. These were men who loved fishing and felt a call of duty to pass the sport on to the young. They did it for no reward and, in all probability, for scant thanks either, I'm afraid. These men put the flesh on the bones of what Mr. Crabtree had originally taught me. It was one thing to see a float set-up in a cartoon but it's another thing to see the technique put into practice in the cold light of a northern dawn. These men taught me how to cast, how to strike, how to play a fish and how to

unhook it. These were the hands-on lessons that the book alone couldn't quite achieve.

These relationships were central to my fishing but they were also important for the way that I grew up from the age of six to at least sixteen or more. Men like Graham, Peter, Ron and the rest taught me to suffer rain, sleet, cold and heat. They taught me how to relate, how to behave and how to grow up.

Finally, as a child, Mr. Crabtree helped me translate the magic of fishing that whirled in my head into the real practice of fishing, generally on a canal bank. Before reading Mr. Crabtree, I'd been simply awestruck by fishing, not knowing where to start or even how to cope with such a vast concept. Mr. Crabtree made fishing more manageable and the book eased me into the way of the waterside. Mr. Crabtree made me think that fishing was there for me, waiting to be discovered and waiting to be understood. I felt Mr. Crabtree was saying to me that the waterside is a massive place, John, but take heart, you will understand it one day. Mr. Crabtree was totally the best companion for all of us then as children.

Now, all those years on, what do I think of Mr. Crabtree? I agree with what Bernard himself said. When he writes that Mr. Crabtree was "innocent", I think he described his creation exactly right. Mr. Crabtree was a bit like Roy of the Rovers or Dixon of Dock Green. He was a man of his times, a man

that a lad could trust. Mr. Crabtree was the real thing with no pretence and, deep down, any reader of any age has somehow picked up on that. For fifteen years, I worked as a teacher and I think Mr. Crabtree even helped me there. Taking his lead, I believed that the most important element in any classroom relationship was sincerity. You've got to be genuine. Kids can sniff out a fake from a mile off and there was nothing fake about Mr. Crabtree.

When Bernard described the writing of Mr. Crabtree he wrote, "I let my loving pleasure run as it would." There has never been a better description of the joy of creativity and it is this that makes Mr. Crabtree so vividly alive. Bernard simply trusted his passion to make Mr. Crabtree work on every level and it shows. Within every cartoon, within every illustration and within every word there is a warmth that comes from the heart. Bernard's love of fishing is a reassurance for us, it's an encouragement for us all to be a part of this magical sport. We all have our own Crabtree moments and mine is this:

For many years, I was passionate about a shoal of barbel on the River Wye. It was possible to view the fish from above with absolute clarity if the weather conditions were right. There were anything up to four hundred fish within the shoal, all forming the tightest of formations. Every one of those barbel would be slightly different in size, shape or colouration so

*Bernard drinking from the source of the Zambezi river.*

they all had an identity. Yet they would entwine in the water, their flanks rubbing together, their fins curling over their neighbour's body. Never before this shoal, had I seen fish so obviously at ease, so obviously taking pleasure in their lives and their comradeship. Perhaps this is the, "loving pleasure," in our watery environment that Bernard so aptly described?

Bernard also wrote that, "Books are objects of trust that should also be beautiful artefacts." We've already discussed the element of trust that Mr. Crabtree gave us but it's also true that the book itself was very beautiful. The glories of nature cannot be improved by anyone but Bernard did come close. Mr. Crabtree Goes Fishing still stands out in the crowd of fishing books in my study because it is so uniquely recognisable. To this day, when I hold my copy, it's electrifying. My Mr. Crabtree is a 1952 second impression – how I'd love a first – and a forensics department would have a field day because my fingerprints must be over every square millimetre. Technically, perhaps because of its landscape layout, the book works beautifully. The mix of watercolours, cartoons and text could not be better balanced or harmonised. It's not often that an instructional book is so pretty and so thrilling to look at.

Today, I realise that Mr. Crabtree fished very much in an idealised environment. Every page in the book reeks of water meadows and willows, wide skies and church steeples. There

are stone bridges and reed-fringed broads and fishermen's boats on waters so intensely brooding that they have inhabited all my dreams since I was a child. Bernard Venables' watercolours stand as a reminder of what our England looked like once upon a time, not very long ago. There are probably deep reasons for this. Bernard certainly wanted to create a watery environment that was entrancing but it's important to remember that Mr. Crabtree came to life very shortly after the end of the Second World War. Bernard wanted to create a land fit for returning angling heroes and every page of Mr. Crabtree shouts out that England was worth fighting, and even dying, for. The thought of Nazis at the Royalty, or Hitler on the Norfolk Broads is just too repulsive to think about.

The 1940s and early '50s were also a period of austerity that we can't even begin to guess at today. When Mr. Crabtree tells Peter how to preserve fish as dead baits he says he used sugar for the purpose once but now, post war, has to make do with formalin. In the cartoon bubble on page 60, Mr. Crabtree is taking Peter to the bream river. He says, "Good ground bait is bread, bran and boiled potato but we must manage with stale bread scraps, sand and boiled potato peelings." Mr. Crabtree's times were tougher than most of us have ever known but at least Bernard could encourage us to rejoice in the English landscape and the wonderful sport of angling. Let's not forget

that Mr. Crabtree first appeared as a long-running series in the Daily Mirror. It's a fact that the Mirror readers were largely urban and Bernard definitely wanted them to realise that there was an English countryside out there worth visiting and preserving.

This is perhaps the biggest thing about Mr. Crabtree that I've come to understand as an adult. Mr. Crabtree taught children to fish and to value fishing but beyond that, he set out to teach every one of us that there is a waterside we need to work very hard to preserve. Mr. Crabtree was written at a time when the environment seemed to be uniquely challenged and Bernard was a true visionary in his ability to see the danger signs way before most. Post Second World War, the country embarked on a period of reconstruction that was, on many levels, environmentally catastrophic. Deep river dredging began in earnest during the Crabtree days and what a disaster that proved to be on every front for the next half century. Bernard was also well aware of the problems of abstraction as the population grew and demands for water rocketed. Pollution also seemed to him an inevitable curse as farming and manufacturing both expanded. Above all, there was the spread of urbanisation that Bernard deeply feared and always doubted would never be controlled in a Crabtree-friendly fashion. Bernard believed that Mr. Crabtree and Peter had witnessed the best of what England had to offer unless we all pledged to help the environment in every way possible.

This is another major reason for my excitement about being involved with Fishing in the Footsteps of Mr. Crabtree. There is a real hope in the new century that things can get better. Anglers truly are guardians of the stream and a healthy sport means healthy fisheries. If we achieve our aim of making fishing a must for a significant percentage of children again, we will have been part of a positive movement that safeguards the aquatic environment far into the future. There exists today a whole stream of organisations doing the sort of work to protect our fisheries that Bernard would have applauded. The Angling Trust, the Environment Agency, the Wild Trout Trust, the Wye and Usk Foundation, the Get Hooked on Fishing Project, and numerous other schemes around the country are doing great work and having a real impact on our fishing future.

As an adult now, I see that Mr. Crabtree is strong on ethics and on why we fish at the most fundamental level. It is no secret that Bernard did not approve of the surge of specimen hunting that swept through the 1960s and '70s and has been rampant ever since. Stillwater Angling, by Richard Walker, is the other main contestant for angling book of the 20th century but Bernard distrusted it. "The technical means and tactics the book taught were faultlessly practical: they did greatly increase the reader's ability to catch fish but imbued an alien spirit. The book led its reader most successfully to the catching of fish but led him away from the philosophical and spiritual delights of angling as an initiation into the rhythm of nature. The spirit of the book was of conquest, of aggressive intent upon fish."

I think we need to remember this in the modern day. All fish are great and any achievement is admirable but fishing isn't all about self, it's about sharing, just like Mr. Crabtree and Peter did. We all like to be Kings or Queens of the river but Mr. Crabtree counsels a more sensitive and sensible attitude. Providing you're there, providing you're part of the whole angling adventure that is the only important thing. It's good to watch Mr. Crabtree and Peter sharing totally in each other's successes, and that is exactly the lesson Bernard wanted to impart.

Today, fifty-odd years from first reading Mr. Crabtree, I realise that Bernard Venables himself was a fascinating, even compelling human being. He was a writer, artist, countryman, prophet, Fleet Street man and adventurer. I have in the past described him as England's answer to Ernest Hemingway and there is a lot of Papa in the drama of Bernard's life. In 1959, for example, he set up a one-man expedition to Madeira where he landed a 1,700 pound shark. In 1966, he was invited by the Zambian government to explore tourism possibilities

there. He even trekked to the source of the Zambezi. In 1967, he went to the islands of the Azores where he went whaling with the locals in small, open boats, as unprotected as those in the days when men hunted Moby Dick. He was over eighty when he fished for tiger fish on Lake Kariba and pursued Nile perch in Uganda. However, unlike Hemingway, Bernard was a more humble man despite his colossal achievements. I remember photographing him at a signing of a new edition of Mr. Crabtree at the CLA Game Fair many years ago. He was genuinely astonished by the queue of Crabtree worshippers that wound around the pavilion and off down Fisherman's Row. For every fan, Bernard had a word and a warm wish and for a Crabtree kid like me, it was in every way a wonderful experience to witness.

I think I got it wrong comparing Bernard to Hemingway and now I rather see him in the vein of one of our country's great, all-round naturalists. Bernard is more akin to the likes of writers like Richard Jefferies, Patrick Chalmers and, perhaps, above all, of Henry Williamson.

I'd like to quote at some length from Hannah Bruford, Bernard's daughter, in her postscript to his biography, A Stream of Life. She writes, "We were surrounded by books, by words and pictures. Outside, we were surrounded by the fields, trees, lanes and ponds. We seemed to spend days wandering through the woods, along tracks, exploring and discovering the natural world. We were taught to appreciate it. We would recognise and name the flowers, the trees, butterflies and birds. We learnt to be still, to really see the natural world. Dad was forever pointing out colours in the landscape or gazing at an impressive sky… "Whilst we were growing up, Mum and Dad were attempting to be organically self-sufficient. We reared chickens, geese and goats and grew vegetables. Our waste was recycled as much as possible and Dad developed an impressive system of compost heaps. This lifestyle slotted into our deeply rural surroundings. We were not shielded from the cycles of the country. We knew the fate of the cute lambs that were born in front of us. The geese that we had to dodge all year were the geese that Dad killed and we plucked for Christmas."

Reading these words made me think instantly of Henry Williamson's classic, A Story of a Norfolk Farm. Here were two men who understood the countryside in its entirety, probably in a way that no-one does today. Perhaps that is another reason why Mr. Crabtree is never far from our minds.

In his last years, Bernard was very much the eco warrior. I can remember listening to him in Northern Ireland one evening explaining why we anglers had to keep on fishing and just how important it is for us to explain to the world at large the good that fishing does.

Here, it is better to quote Bernard himself. "As worms, birds and badgers are animals, so are we. We are of earth, as are all the animals, all the plants. Of earth we are born; by earth we are sustained. We have no independence of earth and that is a gift, if allowed to be, immeasurably lovely. And this we must never cease to acknowledge, every day, for every moment of life, to earth we are bound by an umbilical cord." Fishing the Mr. Crabtree way is not just something to do in life, it is a way of life. Therein lies the power of Crabtree.

Finally, we all have our best Mr. Crabtree story. Donkeys' years ago, I was waiting at Kathmandu airport for a flight back to the UK. That Nepali airport was notoriously dangerous in those days and I remember being even more apprehensive than usual. I was on standby but, at the last moment, missed out on my seat to a luckier passenger. Except he wasn't. The plane took off and flew into the mountainside. There were no survivors.

I was still at the airport and, like everyone else, in a state of shock. I went to a kiosk to buy some chocolate; always a comforter since childhood, and on a shelf behind the vendor was a copy of Mr. Crabtree, there in Nepal all those years ago. I bought it, much to the chap's delight, and I read it all over again, right there in the departure hall. Even in my wretched state of mind, Mr. Crabtree reinforced how utterly fabulous life is. No wonder Bernard Venables was as bright as a hawk until the day he died. Being touched by Mr. Crabtree really is like being dusted with magic.

*Illustration by Bernard Venables from*
*Mr. Crabtree Goes Fishing.*

# MR.CRABTREE

*Illustration by Bernard Venables from*
*Mr. Crabtree Goes Fishing.*

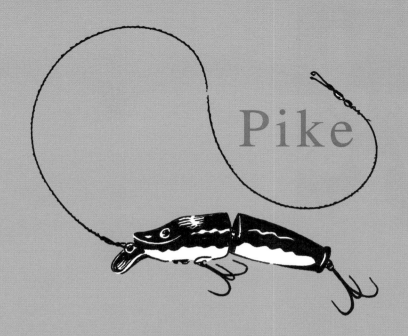

# Pike

"It arises from the powerful image that the pike conjures up. We never know with certainty just how awesomely huge the fish may be, lurking in its watery haunts."

*Bernard Venables M.B.E. - The Illustrated Memoirs of a Fisherman.*

I'd been dreaming along with Mr. Crabtree for a few years when I came across my first, real-life pike. I was wandering my local canal, turned a corner and came across two adult anglers fishing on a dour November afternoon. Hanging from a tree behind them was the fish. Fourteen pounds dead, both in weight and loss of life. I was transfixed. I couldn't understand how a fish of such colossal size could come from such a meagre piece of water. Henceforth in my life, I realised that monsters could always lurk in the shadows, on the very limits of the imagination. Even in death, that fish glowed. The colours, its markings, its fins and its teeth I traced with a quivering finger. Even glazed, the pike's eye seemed to follow me, telling me to be careful, warning me not to mess with such a fish. I didn't like the blood trickling from the fish's gills but that was how pike were treated in those days. I was mesmerised and always would be. Back home, I read how Mr. Crabtree and Peter caught their pike and planned how one day, I'd be doing exactly the same as them.

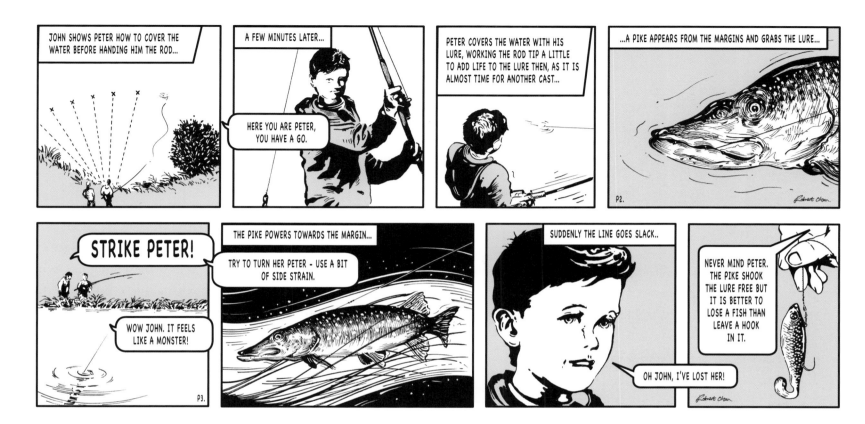

Bernard Venables understood pike very well. When I was young, in Norfolk, the old boys told me that the best pike days were those daylong dark ones when the birds did not sing, exactly as Bernard wrote: "The best of all weathers for pike is the dull, overcast, mild day that comes in winter." However, Bernard also understood that pike are notoriously unpredictable. Whilst pike anglers everywhere pray for gloom, they know that the brightest, coldest, most ice-fringed days can also produce the biggest fish. In short, you never know with pike, happy as they are to break every rule.

Back in Crabtree Time, pike were regarded as an October to March quarry. We are not quite as set on that today. The welfare of the pike is the biggest of all considerations but handled carefully and returned quickly, leaf-on-tree fish don't come to harm. And these warm water pike can be electrifyingly aggressive, hitting lures, sink and draw dead baits and surface

PETER TRIES AGAIN BUT NO LUCK COMES HIS WAY. AFTER HALF AN HOUR JOHN AND PETER TAKE A BREAK TO HAVE A RE-THINK AND JOHN DECIDES TO CHANGE TACTICS AND TO SHOW PETER ANOTHER METHOD OF PIKE FISHING.

WARM YOURSELF UP WITH A CUP OF TEA PETER WHILST I SET UP A DEAD BAIT ROD - WE'LL GIVE THAT A TRY.

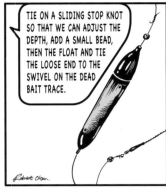

YOUR 12FT CARP ROD WILL DO JUST FINE FOR DEAD BAITING.

I LIKE TO USE A FLOAT. THAT WAY YOU GET AN EARLY INDICATION OF A BITE. BESIDES, I FIND IT MORE EXCITING THAT WAY.

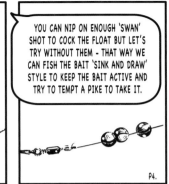

TIE ON A SLIDING STOP KNOT SO THAT WE CAN ADJUST THE DEPTH, ADD A SMALL BEAD, THEN THE FLOAT AND TIE THE LOOSE END TO THE SWIVEL ON THE DEAD BAIT TRACE.

YOU CAN NIP ON ENOUGH 'SWAN' SHOT TO COCK THE FLOAT BUT LET'S TRY WITHOUT THEM - THAT WAY WE CAN FISH THE BAIT 'SINK AND DRAW' STYLE TO KEEP THE BAIT ACTIVE AND TRY TO TEMPT A PIKE TO TAKE IT.

poppers with exhilarating abandon. This is the stuff to get your heart pounding, when you'll be sure to see your own excitement reflected in the face of the young 'Peter' beside you.

If summer piking would be new to Mr. Crabtree so would several other things. The use of salt-water fish dead baits fished static on the bottom or mid-water would have surprised him. He would have found the vast increase in the range of lures used for pike fishing remarkable, and the great strides in pike care and conservation truly heartening. That dead canal pike of mine was how most fish were looked after back then. Not today. Gaffs and gags have long gone to be replaced by unhooking mats, long-nosed pliers, wire cutters and anything that gives the pike a chance to swim away unharmed.

Perhaps that's why there are probably more big pike to be caught today than in Mr. Crabtree's era. More big pike are returned and certainly none today would be considered a candidate for the pot back in Mrs. Crabtree's kitchen. The increase in large gravel pits and reservoirs has also provided

new, spacious homes for monsters. And let's not forget the trout water pike phenomenon that produces more forty pounders in a season than Mr. Crabtree would have expected in a decade.

A perfect pike day has to begin around dawn. As the light grows, it's a great idea to put a couple of dead baits out fished simply under a float. If big distances are required, lead on the line can be used but for most casts, a still-frozen herring or mackerel will be quite heavy and streamlined enough. A couple of SSG shot nipped on the line above the trace are often a good idea but it's rarely necessary to get more complex than that. Set the floats just over depth so the bait rests on the bottom and the piking can begin. Watch for any movement on the float whatsoever and I tend to strike pretty well immediately. My reasoning is that if a pike is large, it will take the bait down fast and an early strike saves deep-hooking, blood and grief. If the pike is small, you might well miss by striking early but you've probably just lost a fish that's more of an irritation than a triumph. A good fish, and I count anything over ten pounds as more than respectable, sets

JOHN SHOWS PETER HOW TO HOOK THE BAIT FOR 'SINK AND DRAW' AND STRESSES THE IMPORTANCE OF USING BARBLESS HOOKS.

P5.

LOOK PETER... SEE THAT GREBE DIVING BY THE REEDS? THERE MUST BE SMALL FISH DOWN THERE SO A PIKE WON'T BE FAR AWAY.

CAST JUST PAST THAT BUSH PETER AND SLOWLY DRAW YOUR BAIT CLOSER TO IT.

AS PETER LIFTS THE ROD AND RETRIEVES SOME LINE THE BAIT RISES...

...AS HE LOWERS THE ROD THE LINE FALLS SLACK AND THE BAIT FLUTTERS BACK DOWN.

you up for the day and, especially if you use barbless hooks, the whole returning process is pain and tear free.

The sun is now rising. Light is flooding into the water and now is the time for a change of tactics. Travel light with an eight-foot spinning rod and a bag of single hook rubber lures and you can work miles of bank before lunchtime. This is the way to get the warmth back into your body and is the kind of fishing to get the adrenaline really pumping. This is where a decent pair of polarised sunglasses will give you a distinct advantage. You'll be able to see the action of your lure as you retrieve it and, very possibly, any pursuing pike. Breathable chest waders are also a good thing, both winter and summer because they allow you to wade the margins and work the lure away from the close-in reed beds.

Though the set-up is simple, the approach is serious. Think about the speed of your retrieve and how to move the lure erratically and enticingly. Think about the depth you are working at and how to cover the whole of the water column

until you make pike contact. Vary the size, the colour and the action of the lure until you find what the pike are taking on any given day. Concentrate hard as you retrieve. Feel for any unexpected bumps or bangs, which are often fish investigating the lure without making any final commitment. The real teasers are those pike that follow the lure right into your feet, threatening an attack without ever actually mounting one. Try hard with these fish: speed the lure up; let it drop to the bottom and twitch; change the lure quickly for a different model that might just provoke a take. I have had thirty pounders play cat and mouse with me like this and fishing just doesn't come more thrilling.

It's good to stop for lunch, especially on a winter's day, when the cold seeps in and you need to take fuel on board. Think hard about what the morning has taught you. Where have you seen the most fish? Have you had any inkling of a particular big fish swirling or following your lure in? Are there any swims that your intuition tells you could be a serious proposition for a

...A VERY TEMPTING SIGHT FOR A HUNGRY PIKE...

SUDDENLY THE FLOAT BOBS...

...AND THEN IT SAILS AWAY.

GET READY PETER... NOW...

...TIGHTEN UP QUICKLY - THEN GIVE A FIRM, STEADY STRIKE TO SET THE HOOKS. WELL DONE PETER - SHE'S ON.

BLIMEY JOHN - SHE CAN'T HALF PULL!

P6. Robert Olsen.

...A GOOD PIKE BY THE WAY SHE IS FIGHTING, TAKE YOUR TIME AND WE'LL GET HER.. THAT'S IT, NICE AND EASY, NOW....

...CAREFUL, DRAW HER IN SLOWLY AND I'LL GET THE NET UNDER HER. YES PETER. WE HAVE HER AND...

...WHAT A WONDERFUL FISH - 17 TO 18LBS FOR SURE.

LET'S GET HER ON THE UNHOOKING MAT AND I'LL SHOW YOU THE BEST WAY TO RELEASE THE HOOKS, THEN WE CAN SLIP HER BACK QUICKLY TO GROW EVEN BIGGER!

I'M STILL SHAKING FROM THE EXCITEMENT! I CAN'T BELIEVE A FISH COULD BE SO STRONG!

Robert Olsen.

P7.

specimen? A bay perhaps, especially if it's deep, sheltered, ringed by trees. It's these sorts of places where you concentrate for the last few hours, before the early dusk of winter. Once again, go back to the floats and the dead baits and be prepared to sit it out for the last two hours of an absorbing day. It's harder to see the floats in the dusk so pay particular care – binoculars are an excellent aid here. Remember that more times than I can remember, the very biggest fish of any day comes just as you are

thinking of packing up, just as the owl is telling you it's time to go home.

I think I have pike fishing in my blood. My grandmother used to tell me about her one and only pike, taken on a small roach that she was reeling in sometime, I guess, around the turn of the 20th century. The marauder stayed clamped on the roach just long enough to allow her fiancé, the grandfather I never knew, to scoop both fish into the net. It was a story that thrilled me to the core and would have a strange, Crabtree-like resonance many years later. I was guiding with a father and an eight-year-old son and we'd just started on the first cast of the day. We were on the Kingfisher Lake and the little chap cast out a lure, which was instantly seized by a jack of a few pounds. I ran to the car just a few yards away to get the net, the unhooking mat and the dentistry tools. When I returned, the father looked puzzled, the child looked alarmed and the rod was menacingly bent. Just like my grandmother's roach almost a century ago, the jack had been seized by a water wolf of massive proportions. I was wearing polarised sunglasses and I could see the battle, deep down, close to our feet in crystal clear water. A pike of not far shy of forty pounds had seized my young client's jack pike and the fight was on. There was a moment, a minute or two later, when the big fish came to the top, the small pike across its jaws. It tail walked half a dozen times, shaking its massive head, flaring its blood-red gills. The child stepped back in appalled, mesmerised horror. The jack flew free, the monster smacked the water's surface. For a minute, none of us spoke. A Crabtree moment isn't always intimate and serene. It can be pulsating, and even brutally exhilarating.

# Unhooking & Pike Safety

Pike look mean but they're actually as vulnerable as any fish and more so than most. When fishing for pike, use a barbless hook if at all possible as these are much kinder to the fish when it comes to unhooking. If possible, too, fish for pike using single hooks as they much more easily extracted than trebles. Always make sure that if you are using dead baits for pike then you strike as quickly as possible. Don't wait for a take to develop overlong as you always run the risk of a pike being more deeply hooked.

If at all possible, try to unhook the pike in the water and avoid taking it onto the bank at all. To do this, you will need long-nosed pliers of at least 12 inches and shallow margins where it is safe to get close to the fish itself.

If, however, a pike is hooked within the mouth and you do need to take it onto the bank to perform the dentistry work, make sure that you always put the pike on a well-wetted, very soft unhooking mat. Never let a pike bounce around on gravel, sand or even grass.

Let's say the dead bait or the lure is well within the pike's mouth. This is how I go about unhooking operations. Let's assume you are right-handed. Lay the pike down and kneel beside it. Lay the fish on its left flank with its head pointing towards your right hand. I generally straddle the fish using my left shin in particular to prevent the fish from flapping. Make sure you don't apply any weight on the fish itself and use the manoeuvre just to keep the fish pinned down and avoid it squirming. If you look under the gill flap of the pike you will see three sets of rakers. Make sure that you avoid these and slide one finger along the gill cover towards the chin where you will find your finger fits perfectly into an area of soft skin where there are no teeth, no rakers and nothing that will potentially damage the pike or yourself.

Lift the pike's head and you will find that its mouth will stay wide open without you using any force on it at all. You will now have the whole mouth cavity opened up to you and you can work without any fear of the mouth closing. Sometimes, a protective glove can give you confidence. Always have a pair of 12-inch forceps and wire snips. Keep the pike wetted throughout so you will need a bucket of water close by.

The wire cutters can be useful if the hooks are secured in a tricky position. Sometimes it's best just to destroy the hooks rather than try to remove them whole. Never cut the wire as all you are doing is condemning the pike to a slow death.

With the pike in this position and with the unhooking tools at hand, you should find that the hooks will come out easily and the whole process should never take more than a minute.

If there are problems, don't panic. Put the fish back in the water to rest while you have a breather. It could be that someone close to you on the bank is a little more experienced and never be afraid of asking for their help. Remember that if the pike begins to go pale, then it is suffering from stress and you need to get it back into the water immediately.

Presuming the unhooking goes well, either carry the pike back to the water in both hands or put it in the net for the short journey back to the margins. Once the fish is in the water, use your left hand to support the head and use your right hand to hold the tail root but don't grip the tail with any force. All you are doing is balancing the fish. Don't let an exhausted pike swim away immediately. Retain it until you are quite sure it has recovered all of its strength. This is particularly important when you are fishing a river.

Never fish for pike until you are confident you can unhook them. Go out with experienced anglers until you are sure that you are confident on your own. Courses on pike unhooking are often held around the country. Your club might organise this or the Pike Anglers Club of Great Britain is sure to have seminars locally.

Be confident. Don't panic. Don't be afraid. Have all the right tools. Know the right unhooking positions. Keep the fish out of the water for as little time as possible. Tick all of these boxes and all of your pike should go back safely every time.

*Illustration by Bernard Venables from*
*Mr. Crabtree Goes Fishing.*

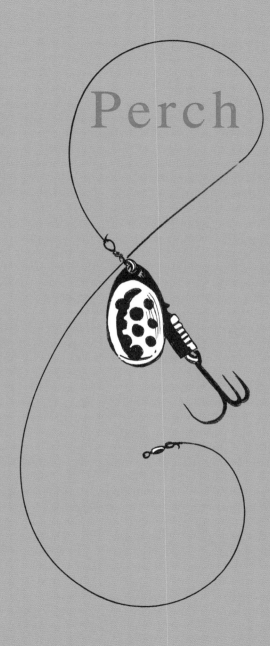

# Perch

"The perch, it has always been said, is the beginner's fish, the maker of anglers. Just let one boy, or the previously non-fisherman, draw from under the water one perch, one perch of whatever size, so the story runs, and the spell will be upon him."

*Bernard Venables M.B.E. - Mr. Cherry Series.*

Bernard Venables was of the opinion that many young anglers were set on the road to a fishing life because of the glamour and catchability of the perch. When I was starting out, Crabtree obsessed, it certainly was the perch that did it for me. One Saturday, summer morning on the Macclesfield canal, a small perch came from the depths of the boat channel, up onto the shallow towpath margin and, in frozen time, engulfed the worm fished by my equally tiny comrade. The little fish was hauled into the sunlight and we were captivated by its colours, its bars, its fins and its entire bristling defiance. It was the first time, I think, I'd experienced unquenchable envy. It took me a while to realise my own perching time would come. Shortly after, I joined a club with the rights to a small mill reservoir which was, fortunately, Crabtree-crystal-clear. My holidays and my weekends could be spent watching exactly how perch behaved, how they approached my worms, how their fins splay out, rock-erect. I loved their pugnacity, their feistiness, the way they bossed every cupful of water in that little reservoir. In time,

JOHN AND PETER BY THE EDGE OF A LOVELY LAKE...

HAVE A LOOK IN MY BAG FOR A BOX OF LITTLE SPINNERS PETER AND I'LL SET UP THE ROD.

I'VE SET UP A LIGHT 10FT SPINNING ROD WITH 8LB LINE ON A LITTLE FIXED SPOOL REEL - THAT SHOULD DO NICELY...

Robert Olsen.

..A SMALL MEPPS TYPE SPINNER IS GOOD FOR PERCH. I HAVE ATTACHED A WIRE TRACE BECAUSE THERE ARE A FEW PIKE IN HERE TOO!

PH1.

PERCH USUALLY LIE CLOSE TO COVER SO START BY TRYING TO BRING THE LURE PAST THOSE REEDS...

I learnt how to catch the bigger perch there which could make the reel sing and the rod bend but I never lost my affection for the two ouncers, the little bad lads of the pond.

If you read the original text, you will realise there is a shadow over Mr. Crabtree's perch fishing. Bernard believed that first rate perching was, "a thing of the past." In the late 1940s Bernard was understandably worried about pollution, abstraction and bad river management but he could not have foreseen the disasters of the so-called Perch Disease that decimated perch

stocks in the Sixties, Seventies and even into the Eighties. As a young man, I can remember the devastation that PD wrought. The scene on a Norfolk gravel pit will never leave me. I was actually fishing for perch that October day, facing into a brisk wind. Perch between two and a half and three and a half pounds were coming to the surface in front of me, ulcerated, floundering, dying at my feet. It was the most appalling, sickening, devastating of experiences. I was heartbroken to see my beloved perch die in this tragic, meaningless fashion.

WE NEED TO GET TO THAT LAKE EARLIER NEXT TIME PETER. WE MUST HAVE CAUGHT THE PERCH RIGHT AT THE END OF THEIR FEEDING PERIOD.

WE COULD USE THE SAME SPINNER YOU CAUGHT THAT FISH ON THIS MORNING BUT LET'S TRY FLOAT FISHING. A FLOAT WILL ALLOW US TO USE THE CURRENT TO SEARCH OUT A FISH.

THIS WEIR POOL LOOKS AS THOUGH IT COULD BE STUFFED WITH FISH... CAN WE HAVE A GO NOW JOHN?

AS IS OFTEN THE CASE, SIMPLE TACKLE IS ALL YOU NEED - A 'CHUBBER' FLOAT WITH ENOUGH SHOT TO COCK IT.

WHAT BAIT ARE WE GOING TO USE JOHN?

WELL, THERE IS NO FINER PERCH BAIT THAN A BIG LOBWORM - A TOTALLY NATURAL BAIT - ON THE RIGHT DAY PERCH JUST CAN'T SEEM TO RESIST THEM!

JOHN SHOWS PETER HOW TO HOOK THE WORM AND THEN CASTS INTO THE HEAD OF THE WEIR POOL AND LETS THE CURRENT TAKE THE FLOAT. HE THEN SHOWS PETER HOW TO CONTROL THE LINE SO THAT THE FLOAT CAN BE GUIDED DOWN THE RUN. PETER HAS A GO AND SOON GETS THE HANG OF IT.

THAT'S IT. LET THE CURRENT TAKE THE FLOAT BUT KEEP MENDING THE LINE TO KEEP IN CONTACT WITH IT...

..TRY TO GUIDE IT CLOSER TO THOSE OVERHANGING LEAVES...

LOOK JOHN, MY FLOAT'S GOING!

WAIT A MOMENT, PERCH OFTEN SUCK A WORM IN AND THEN BLOW IT OUT AGAIN BEFORE TAKING IT PROPERLY...

IT'S GONE!

...NOW QUICKLY, TIGHTEN UP THE LINE AND THEN...

PH5.

Blessedly for all of us, perch have made a magnificent comeback since those dark days. I guess there are now more perching opportunities than there have been in my life before. I can think of perch waters all around the country with spanking new stocks of these fine fish. Perch of a pound abound everywhere and two pounders and even three pounders are far from uncommon. One of my great fishing friends, Neill, recently broke the record with a six pound plus monster. And how about this story of mine to fire the blood? A year ago, in crystal water beneath a bridge, a friend of mine played a perch that was to weigh three pounds six ounces. On its way up through the water column this cracking perch was itself seized by a monster, a great, striped leviathan that appeared from nowhere. The massive perch turned the three pounder and began to swallow, only being thwarted by the sail-like, erect dorsal of the struggling smaller fish. The attack lasted for some minute or so and, I would say, hand on heart, the marauding monster had to be at least twice the size of the fish that we eventually landed and weighed.

If that doesn't fire you up to be a perch fisherman, then nothing will.

There's one marvellous thing about perch fishing today. In every way, it resembles the perch fishing of Mr. Crabtree's day. The perch story is the last cartoon strip in the book and Mr Crabtree and Peter catch perch on float and worm, possibly my first approach today. And, the last bubble in the book says this... "You can catch perch on minnows and small gudgeon as well as worms and it's good fun to spin for them with a thread line outfit and a small artificial bait. You can even catch them on a wet fly." Exactly. Unlike some fish species, the perch remains true to Crabtree. Really, if Mr. Crabtree and Peter trod our perch waters today, there is barely anything we could teach them.

Instead, let Mr. Crabtree teach us. He took the time to sit, chew on his pipe and watch the water around him and that's one of Crabtree's most important lessons. Rush is not a word great anglers use. Control and patience are the keys and, following this route, Mr. Crabtree absorbed just about everything there is to

know about the lifestyle of the perch.

We can also learn from Mr. Crabtree and Peter through their phrase, "Mobility and freedom." That is the Crabtree way of fishing that I have never personally shaken off. I don't like to do dull. Life is for fishing and not for rusting away. If you keep working throughout your perch day, Crabtree-style, you will be tired, exhausted and exhilarated by the end. And, thankfully, there is nothing hi-tech about any of this. Perch fishing has always been simple and should be kept so.

It's a first consideration that if you want to be a fisherman and see the best of the day, it's good to have an alarm clock. The best of perch fishing, too, is not much after dawn, winter or summer. This is when perch, in stillwaters especially, are truly out and about, foraging for breakfast, particularly catchable. Like Mr. Crabtree always was, it's good to keep mobile. Artificial lures are perfect for this game. The little silver Mepps spinners that Mr. Crabtree would have used are still perfect but, more often today, we'll probably use small plastic lures and especially jigs.

The lightest of rods and small fixed spool reels with six pound breaking strain line are just about perfect. If there are pike about, you will probably need a wire trace and step up that breaking strain a little.

Hunt for your perch wherever you might see surface action. Pike tend to boil at prey shoals, striking indiscriminately whilst perch will pursue a single victim over several yards of water. If there is no surface action, however, then you've got to search out where the fish like to live. Overhanging trees are amongst my favourites but I also like any manmade structures like boat bays, piers, or especially bridges and their supports. Look for perch in bays, around feeder streams and anywhere the prey fish themselves like to collect. Work those jigs with every scrap of imagination you possess. Remember that takes aren't always crash, bang, wallop affairs but sometimes you will just get the merest sensation of the jig being mouthed. It often pays to give just a little slack line for a second or two before striking. If you're using Mepps, remember red wool around the treble

doesn't half pull the perch in.

Lure fishing, whichever lure you choose, is always thrilling because it's mobile, keeps you thinking and keeps you experimenting. If one lure isn't working, then take it off and try another and another and another until you find the winning combination. But never stop working at it. Keep going until you find the perch and you earn your rewards.

If the artificials aren't working, then it's time to use real bait and, in my book – just like Mr. Crabtree's book - the perch like nothing better than a worm. Fish one under a float, slow-sinking in exactly the sort of places you'd be working your lure. Watch out for good, big, positive bites and give a second before stiking firmly. Sometimes it pays to free feed around the float with maggots or chopped worms but, frequently, especially in clear water, a big lobworm on its own on a size 8 or 6 hook is all you're going to need. My advice is to put the shot up the line towards the float, so the worm sinks slowly through the water column by its own weight alone. Fish slightly over depth so the worm hovers on or around the bottom and twitch the float from time to time to give the bait extra life.

Now, it's down to the river. Exactly as Mr. Crabtree said, you investigate any likely perch areas. Weir pools, though, are my own magic places. I've learnt that very frequently big perch don't come instantly to the bait. You've often got to work to overcome their suspicion and to get them on the feed. My favourite approach, these days, is to fish a stick float set a few inches off the bottom and begin with three maggots on a size 14 hook. I'll look for a nice, steady run out of the main current but away from the slack water, too. I don't want fast and I don't want extreme depth… I want the medium-paced water in between. If this flows over a clean, gravel bottom, exactly as Mr. Crabtree advised, so much the better.

I won't panic if I've fished for anything up to an hour without success. I'll keep feeding and I'll know that the more I feed, the more likely it is that the big perch will come out to play. If I'm getting pestered with small fish like minnows and gudgeon it's very possible that the big perch aren't in the area but once the small fry disappear, though, it's really time to concentrate. The float buries, the strike hits a solid, sullen, tip-jagging resistance and you know you're in big perch business. See a two or three pounder come towards the daylight, always battling to regain the depths, and it's one of the great sights in angling. You'll be glad that you got up early and you will want to stay out late. As I said, a full day's perch fishing is exhilarating and exhausting in equal parts.

Finally, never forget small, natural dead baits. A dead gudgeon – if you chance upon one – is probably as fine a perch bait as ever existed. Let it trundle down with the river's current. Twitch it back. Let it fall to the bottom. Let it drift downriver, especially under trees or along the roots of reed beds. Fish it around bridge supports, in and out of eddies, just anywhere you suspect a big perch may be lying in ambush. Small roach are just about as good and if you can't get those but come across a tiny dead perch, you'll find just how cannibalistic the species is.

"Perch fishing is a stirring sport," said Mr. Crabtree to Peter. He never got it wrong.

*Illustration by Bernard Venables from*
*Mr. Crabtree Goes Fishing.*

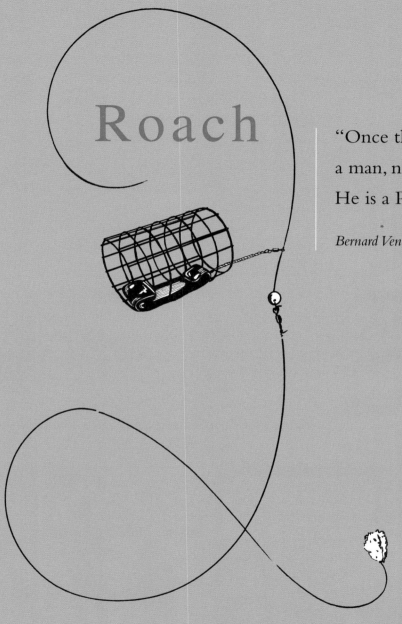

# Roach

"Once the spell of Roach fishing has settled on a man, no other fish can draw him from his love. He is a Roach fisherman for life."

*Bernard Venables M.B.E. - Mr. Crabtree Goes Fishing.*

It's hard for me to describe the multi-layered magic of roach fishing in the black and white days of the north-western 1950s. All my fishing, in my very earliest years, was on the canals and my constant dreams were of the most popular fish of the day, the red-finned, red-eyed roach. So popular was the roach after the Second World War that Bernard Venables devotes two and a half sections to this species in Mr. Crabtree - not even pike has as much as that.

There were so many roach wizards in the Greater Manchester area for me to learn from and perhaps the best times of all were the long summer evenings, especially the holidays when I was allowed to stay out later. Then, those men would come to the canals after their mill shift, so confident in their ability, seemingly fishing with magic in their every movement, miraculous to a lad like me. Their banter mingled with the cigarette smoke and the hum of the midges. I always remember the evenings as warm, with the women taking in washing, talking over fences, watching their men-folk while away the

JOHN AND PETER MEET BY THE BRIDGE...

IT'S PRETTY GREY AND LOOKS AS THOUGH IT MIGHT RAIN JOHN, BUT CAN WE STILL GO FISHING?

WELL PETER, WE'VE GOT OUR WATERPROOFS ON, AND IT'S STILL MILD, SO WE STAND A GOOD CHANCE OF CATCHING SOME ROACH.

IT'S QUITE A WALK BUT I KNOW A GOOD PLACE WHERE A SIDE-STREAM RUNS IN THROUGH A LITTLE SLUICE... THE ROACH OFTEN CONGREGATE THERE.

HERE WE ARE - LET'S TRY FISHING WITH MAGGOTS...

...A LITTLE STICK FLOAT WILL ALLOW US TO SEARCH THE WATER.

BREADFLAKE IS WORTH A GO TOO, IT'S A FINE BAIT FOR BIG ROACH.

A CENTREPIN WITH 2 - 3LB LINE IS A GREAT WAY TO FISH A LITTLE RIVER LIKE THIS ONE.

KEEP CATAPULTING A FEW MAGGOTS IN EACH TIME I RUN THE FLOAT DOWN PETER. THAT WAY THE HOOK BAIT APPEARS MORE NATURAL TO THE FISH AND GETS THEM COMPETING FOR THE FOOD.

AFTER 15 MINUTES WITHOUT A BITE JOHN TRIES HOLDING THE FLOAT BACK A LITTLE AND...

AS A FISH TAKES THE RISING BAIT HE MAKES A GENTLE STRIKE...

THE FISH TRIES TO GET INTO THE WEED BUT IT DOESN'T TAKE LONG FOR JOHN TO TURN IT...

YES! WE HAVE ONE - BUT IT'S DOESN'T FEEL LIKE A BIG FISH.

AS THE ROACH IS GENTLY LANDED JOHN IS PROVED RIGHT...

WELL, IT'S A LOVELY LOOKING ROACH AND IT IS GREAT TO SEE THAT THE YOUNGER FISH ARE COMING ON BUT IT'S NOT REALLY THE GRANDMOTHER I WAS HOPING FOR - STILL, LET'S TRY AGAIN WITH A PINCH OF BREADFLAKE THIS TIME, A CHANGE OF BAIT MAY TEMPT A BIGGER FISH.

twilight. Often there would be a few pence wagered on the evening's roaching outcome and the fishing would always come to an end a good hour before the pub closed its doors.

I was twelve before I could compete on any level against these mill-working maestros for only then had I been taught the simple basics of catching good roach. You don't disturb the fish. You present the bait – generally maggot or caster in those days – as perfectly as possible. That's about it, the secret of roach fishing for all of us to this day. I was taught to fish a float on the lightest of lines with the tiniest of hooks and the most meagre of scatterings of bait tight in the swim. The float could be a crow quill weighing absolutely nothing. Best of all was the summer I came under the wing of a visiting French angler, working on dye-fixing improvements in one of the mills. He taught me to fish a matchstick, each night picked fresh from the canal towpath – and attached by rubbers top and bottom. His English was questionable but his lessons were plain as a pikestaff and my skills rocketed to such an extent I became confident I could catch

JOHN FISHES ON BUT ONLY HOOKS ONE ROACH ON BREADFLAKE THAT SLIPS THE HOOK JUST AS PETER IS ABOUT TO SLIDE THE NET UNDER IT. IT'S OBVIOUS THAT A CHANGE OF LOCATION AND TACTICS ARE NEEDED SO THEY GATHER UP THE TACKLE AND MOVE DOWN THE RIVER TO A PLACE JOHN SUSPECTS MAY HOLD SOME BETTER FISH...

FURTHER DOWN RIVER...

IT LOOKS LIKE A DIFFICULT PLACE TO FLOAT FISH JOHN!

I'LL SET UP A QUIVERTIP ROD FOR YOU PETER AND WE'LL LEDGER WITH A LITTLE PINCH OF BREADFLAKE.

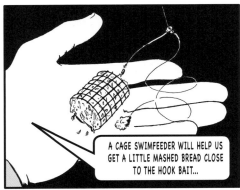

A CAGE SWIMFEEDER WILL HELP US GET A LITTLE MASHED BREAD CLOSE TO THE HOOK BAIT...

PETER CASTS OUT TO AN AREA WHERE JOHN SUSPECTS THE ROACH MAY BE TEMPTED TO FEED AND SCATTERS A LITTLE MASHED BREAD UPSTREAM SO THAT IT TRICKLES DOWN WITH THE CURRENT...

THAT'S IT PETER, TIGHTEN THE LINE AND PUT THE ROD IN THE REST SO THERE'S A LITTLE BEND IN THE QUIVERTIP

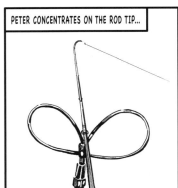

PETER CONCENTRATES ON THE ROD TIP...

roach out of a bucket. I understood that roach fell into traps no heavier than the gossamer of a spider's web. I was into the roach and I was into the mill-workers' money. These are lessons I've never forgotten and never replaced. Above all, they are simple lessons. The most basic one being that if you spook the roach then you will just never catch it.

For twenty years, from the start of the 1970s to the end of the '80s, my roach fishing took on a dreamlike quality all of its own. I was fishing the rivers of East Anglia and the roach

in them were simply huge. Now I was fishing much more like Mr. Crabtree and Peter on that swollen river at the start of the book. The float was now replaced with the lead and the size 20 or even 22 hook became an 8 or a 10. My roaching now was all butt indicator or quivertip work, nearly always at night, nearly always on a big, slack bend with bread flake fished hard on the bottom.

The rewards, in the roach hall of fame, were gobsmacking. In the north a colossal roach was four ounces: now, I was

BENEATH THE SURFACE A GROUP OF ROACH HAVE BEEN ATTRACTED BY THE LITTLE PIECES OF BREAD TRUNDLING DOWN WITH THE CURRENT. IT TAKES A WHILE BECAUSE THEY ARE VERY CAUTIOUS THEN...

THE TEMPTATION BECOMES TOO MUCH AND A FISH TAKES PETER'S BAIT...

WOW, PETER! STRIKE!

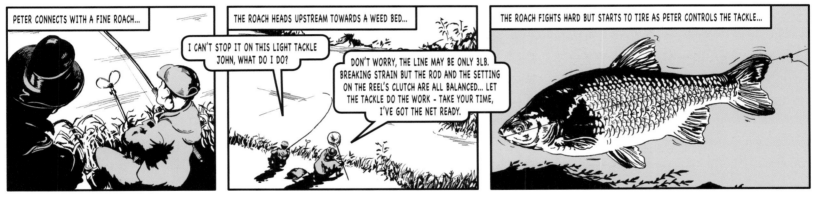

PETER CONNECTS WITH A FINE ROACH...

I CAN'T STOP IT ON THIS LIGHT TACKLE JOHN, WHAT DO I DO?

THE ROACH HEADS UPSTREAM TOWARDS A WEED BED...

DON'T WORRY, THE LINE MAY BE ONLY 3LB. BREAKING STRAIN BUT THE ROD AND THE SETTING ON THE REEL'S CLUTCH ARE ALL BALANCED... LET THE TACKLE DO THE WORK - TAKE YOUR TIME, I'VE GOT THE NET READY.

THE ROACH FIGHTS HARD BUT STARTS TO TIRE AS PETER CONTROLS THE TACKLE...

weighing fish eight, ten, twelve times as big. This was roach fishing in Jurassic Park. The fishing was easy in some ways but hard in others. Presentation, for example, was one dimensional in its simplicity but locating the roach was a matter of extreme angling detective work. The rivers, then, held very few big fish indeed, even though they were leviathans. Tracking them down was a hunter's task that would have made Davy Crockett proud. The fishing, too, was Crabtree exciting. As the daylight faded to give way to dusk, the whole aspect of the flood plains changed.

The advent of the owl, the mists and the blackness lent roach fishing a mystery that I'd never experienced before. When a big, no colossal, roach rolled out in front of me on those black nights, my excitement was perhaps as great as it's ever been in fishing. And when the bobbin flicked, lifted and gathered pace, hammering to the butt, nothing has ever been more heart stopping.

Mr. Crabtree taught Peter to fish with the float and that, for the last fifteen years is how I have come to think roach fishing

really should be. My nights of ambush techniques have given way to the quest to achieve the roach float perfection that Mr. Crabtree set out to teach Peter. Over these years, I've relearned my northern lessons and have added to them the experience of roach fishing on a score of rivers around the country since. First and foremost, Mr. Crabtree was right. You have to fish the right float for the conditions. That matchstick float on the northern canals would be totally out of place in the deep, clear, gushing water of the Hampshire Avon. Equally, that big, cork-bodied float necessary on the Avon would frighten the fins off a Wensum fish. That's the basic law and it's a simple one. Match the float to the flow and you are halfway there.

The second element is feeding. As a lad from the north and as a young man from East Anglia, I was initially flabbergasted by the amount of feed that the best Avon roach men fed into their swims. For me, in East Anglia, a couple of slices of bread would probably suffice for a session. These guys were using loaves. By the same token my two slices of bread would have seemed a lot

on some of the northern canals, especially in the winter when the going was desperately hard. You will never get it all right, but get some of it nearly there and you're halfway to being a roach man.

My perfect roaching day would take place sometime between November and March in relatively mild, relatively quiet conditions. I'd choose one of our smaller typically English rivers, something like my beloved Wensum. And I'd get out there at dawn, as light is breaking, when the roach love to roll in the steady, composed, impressive boils that I have learned to recognise at a quarter of a mile or more.

I'd try to choose a swim that faces east. That way, you will see the river light up downstream of you and you can watch for the big fish rolling in the face of the rising sun. Your red-tipped float turns to black against the ever-lightening water and, when it buries and when you strike into that heavy, brooding resistance, you know exactly how Peter felt the first time he was attached to a roach.

A smaller river allows you to fish a stick float top and bottom with relatively small shot strung down the line. Maggots have to be a favourite bait in clear water but, if there's a cloud to it because of heavy rain, bread flake, once again, is impossible to beat. Personally, I find it hard to fish for roach with a rod over thirteen feet in length. I was brought up on eleven or twelve foot rods at the most and I'm used to something shorter than the fourteen and fifteen foot rods often in vogue today. I sincerely believe, just like Mr. Crabtree, that hand-on-heart

you cannot trot for roach successfully in a river without using a centrepin. Of course, a fixed spool reel can do the job but nowhere near as effectively. Watch a man fish a fixed spool and he always looks clumsy, clunky, as though he's not in total oneness with the flow. If you master the centrepin, even if for this one style of fishing alone, I promise you will never regret it. Your control will be so perfect, your sense of feel so total. You will know exactly what the current is doing, your strike will be perfect and you will play the roach with a sensitivity unknown

PETER MAKES SEVERAL CASTS TO THE PLACE JOHN HAS POINTED OUT SO HE CAN GET A LITTLE CARPET OF BAIT THAT THEY HOPE WILL ENTICE THE ROACH. HE THEN MAKES HIMSELF COMFORTABLE AS HE CONCENTRATES ON THE QUIVERTIP FOR THE SLIGHTEST MOVEMENT... AS THE SUN BEGINS TO SINK THERE ARE STILL NO BITES SO JOHN ATTACHES A 'STARLIGHT' TO THE QUIVER AND URGES PETER TO FISH THROUGH AS THE DUSK DESCENDS OVER THE LAKE....

HALF AN HOUR PASSES BEFORE PETER'S TIP TWITCHES A COUPLE OF TIMES AND THEN PULLS AROUND...

YES! GOT ONE... IT'S PULLING HARD JOHN - I THINK IT MIGHT BE A TENCH!

WELL, THERE ARE CERTAINLY TENCH IN THIS LAKE PETER BUT THE ROACH IN HERE FIGHT WELL ABOVE THEIR WEIGHT ON LIGHT TACKLE - EITHER WAY, TAKE YOUR TIME - YES! IT'S A ROACH, I CAN SEE IT NOW, NICE FISH TOO!

FINALLY THE ROACH IS IN THE NET...

THE WAIT WAS WORTHWHILE PETER, WHAT A CRACKING LOOKING ROACH - WELL DONE...

I'LL SLIP HER BACK WHILST YOU MAKE ANOTHER CAST - THE ROACH ARE OBVIOUSLY FEEDING IN THIS FADING LIGHT.

PETER CATCHES TWO MORE ROACH BEFORE THE BITES DRY UP AND JOHN SUGGESTS THEY CALL AN END TO THE DAY.

I WOULD FISH EVERY DAY OF THE WEEK IF I DIDN'T HAVE TO GO TO SCHOOL JOHN!

QUITE A DAY PETER, A BIG RIVER ROACH AND THREE GOOD ONES FROM THE LAKE - JUST GOES TO SHOW THAT SOME OF THE DULLEST LOOKING DAYS CAN BE THE BEST FOR FISHING!

to the fixed spool angler. This isn't wizardry or witchcraft. It's what Mr. Crabtree taught and the lesson has never been bettered.

Learn to hold the float back so that the shot and, crucially, the hook bait lifts up from the bottom and wavers enticingly in the current. Learn to mend the line so that the float follows its trot without being dragged off course. Fish the float slightly over depth so it trundles along, bumping bottom, lifting up when held back, exploring that vital hand span above the river bed. That is where the biggest roach of all choose their feeding zone.

If you feed cleverly, enough to keep them interested and not so much you overfeed them, you might keep the roach in the swim until lunchtime or beyond.

If I can't get down to the river at dawn, then I'll try to arrive in the late afternoon and, once again, I'll trot a swim as far into dusk as my eyesight will allow. It's at this point that a sort of sixth-sense takes over. You can't quite be sure whether the float is there or whether it has been pulled under but once you're in tune with your roach, a little voice will tell you when to strike

or when to keep the trot going. Don't worry about this.
Again, it's just a sign of being in touch with what the river is
telling you.

When Bernard wrote about the adventures of Mr. Crabtree
and Peter, he knew that our river systems would be facing great
challenges in the later 20th century. What he couldn't know was
that possibly of all the species, roach would suffer amongst the
most. There are many reasons that roach populations began to
decline cataclysmically from the 1970s but perhaps dredging,
which Bernard alludes to in the original book, was the most
serious culprit. The dredger took away the roach spawning beds
and, most vitally, left the smaller fish no shelter in the winter
floods. The small roach could be washed downriver, through
mills sometimes, all the way to the sea.

Today, we live in far more enlightened times and I am so
happy that rivers all around the country are now beginning
to be treated as they should be, with sensitivity and with
understanding. All of our species are responding to this new
approach but it is the roach, especially, that is reviving as river
restoration schemes gather pace. It is my guess that new anglers
are soon going to find many rivers offering them the type of
sport that Mr. Crabtree and Peter enjoyed. This is vital to the
future of fishing because trotting the float is just about the most
satisfying and simply effective skill that there is in angling and,
really, must never be lost.

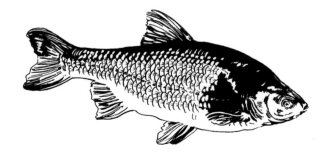

# Watercraft Stillwaters

Stillwaters are not as easy to read as rivers at first glance, but you will soon begin to recognise the signs that are important. Look especially for shallow areas set amidst the deeps. Islands are always worth checking out, as are bays and any inflowing feeder streams. Take note of the wind direction and of banks that are shaded by trees. Water weed is vital and you will often find fish in the densest of these, especially in hot weather.

Finally, remember stillwaters are never still. The winds always have an effect upon them and there will be underwater currents on all our lakes whether large or small.

*Illustration by Bernard Venables from*
*Mr. Crabtree Goes Fishing.*

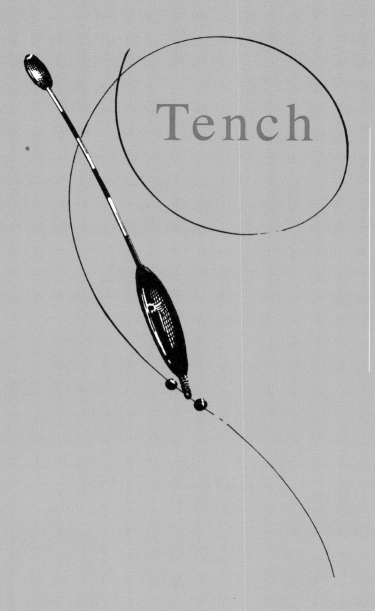

# Tench

"There is no doubt that these early days of the season are the golden time for Tench. And there could be no more delightful way of opening the season than this. Those perfect, pearly mornings and serene, slowly sinking evenings are the very essence that justifies for fishing the title of "the contemplative mans recreation.""

*Bernard Venables M.B.E. - Mr. Crabtree Goes Fishing.*

Late in his life, I was fortunate enough to talk to Bernard himself in a perfect Mr. Crabtree setting. We were in a castle in Northern Ireland with a large fire burning and a glass of brandy to hand. We were talking about his long life in fishing and the species that had given him the most pleasure. Tench kept bubbling to the surface and I felt then that it had been those blissful, summer mornings on stunning stillwaters that had brought him the most pleasure, or certainly the richest memories. The tench is so quintessentially an English fish and I guess that is why we so adore them. There is no better description than Bernard's of the tench and he reminded me of it that night. "The fatly amber tench," says just about everything you need to know about this adorable English fish.

It was Mr. Crabtree's adventures that made me burn to get to grips with tench many years ago and at long last, my morning came. It began badly, though. It was one of those high summer days that you could easily be fooled into thinking was early spring. The clouds were low, there was a sneaky wind from the

EARLY MORNING AT A SECLUDED LAKE...

WE'RE IN WITH A GOOD CHANCE OF A TENCH THIS MORNING PETER. I'VE BEEN BAITING AN AREA JUST OFF THIS DAM WALL WITH MINI PELLETS AND SWEETCORN FOR THE LAST COUPLE OF DAYS.

WHAT A BEAUTIFUL LAKE!

KEEP AS QUIET AS YOU CAN PETER, WE'RE FISHING CLOSE TO THE BANK AND ANY NOISE WILL ALERT THE FISH - I'LL SET UP TWO 13FT. FLOAT RODS WHILST YOU GET YOURSELF COMFORTABLE.

BECAUSE WE'RE FISHING CLOSE IN WE'LL USE CENTREPINS WITH 6LB LINE, THEY ARE SUCH LOVELY REELS TO FISH FOR TENCH WITH.

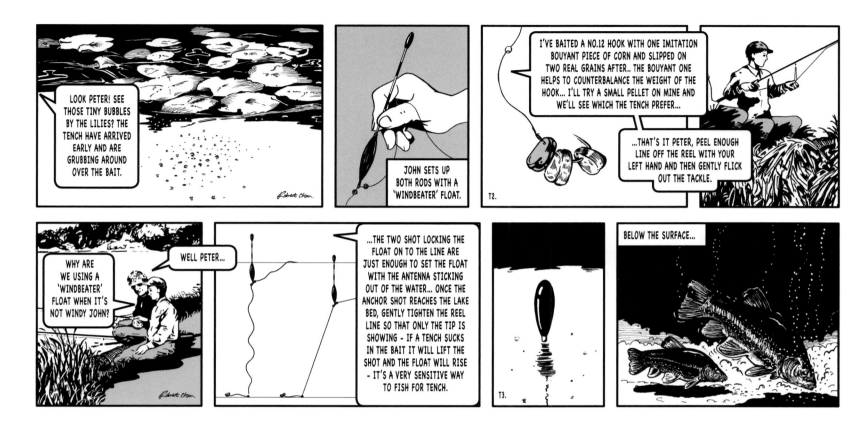

north and there was rain in the air. I was fishing North Norfolk's magnificent Holkham Lake, though its grandeur was totally lost on me, so focused was I on my swim, the reeds and my little red, favourite, crow quill float. Around nine a.m. it moved deliberately and slowly to the right, dipping all the while. Even after fifty years I can remember every detail, like yesterday, just as if I were living my own Crabtree cartoon.

But I was hopelessly out of my depth. The power of the fish was completely beyond my ability. For thirty seconds I hung on,

had the tiger by its tail but inevitably the line parted, thankfully beneath rather than above my beloved float. I was downcast. My heart was in my boots. My life was destined for failure.

At eleven – I've always kept a fishing diary, so I know the details – the clouds lifted a tad. There was even a little bleak sunshine forcing its way through. I made my way round to the dam, which still exists on this wonderful lake. I sat hunched up, lost in my despair, when the float, once again, trundled to the right. This time, in much deeper water, the tench didn't run

as much as plug away down on the bottom. This gave me the time to muster my meagre fish-fighting resources and within five minutes, the fatly amber fish was rolling towards my small, triangular landing net and, with a scoop of triumph, it was mine. Now my heart had wings and my life had promise.

A lot has changed in the tenching world since that morning and since Mr. Crabtree's day but, still, much remains the same. We still like to think of the tench as a fish of the warm months, of wonderful stillwaters where the wood pigeons sing. We like to think of tench fishing as the dawn steals in and the mists begin to rise. We like to think of serene, placid lakes, their surfaces broken only by slowly porpoising tench and clusters of rising, pinprick bubbles. We like to think of tench fishing close in, by reed beds or lilies, preferably with a float. We like to think of those floats bobbing, curtseying, sliding into invisibility. There is no better way to catch a tench.

But, equally, we have to say that a lot has changed. The abolition of the closed season on stillwaters has meant that tench fishing now takes place in April and May and is probably at its height before the traditional opening on June 16th. We have to admit, too, that carp-like methods have crept into tenching. Now, more and more of us fish at range with maggot feeder rigs and often with leads and boilies.

Our tench, too, have grown bigger. The record in Mr. Crabtree's day was not much over seven pounds. Into my thirties, I still yearned for a six pounder. Today, I probably wouldn't even weigh such a fish. In large part, this extraordinary change has come about because of the gravel pits. Mr. Crabtree and Peter fished exclusively for tench in estate lakes and farm ponds, like we all did. Nowadays, ninety-odd percent of tench, I guess, come from the gravel pits that date from the 1940s when Mr. Crabtree was first being realised. There are still estate lake tench but, in the modern age, these have become the minority. It's on the bigger, deeper, more windswept gravel pits that the modern-day tencher frequently has to look.

As it happened, when we filmed Fishing in the Footsteps of Mr. Crabtree, in May 2012, both the traditional and the modern ways of tenching were played out, side-by-side, separated only by a large willow tree. It was the second day of the two-day shoot. I was set up to the left-hand side of the willow with a thirteen-foot float rod, centrepin and waggler. I was fishing, Crabtree-like, a few inches over depth with maggots as bait. The only aspect of what I was doing that might have struck Mr. Crabtree as strange, was the fact that I had plastic, buoyant, imitation maggots on the

hook rather than real ones. The purpose of these, simply, is to counteract the weight of the hook and give the offering much needed buoyancy. Apart from that, I was fishing as Crabtree as you like.

On the other side of the willow tree, in a bigger, more open swim, I'd placed my protégé, Sam. I'd fixed him up with two modern maggot inline feeder rigs, placed on rod rests and buzzers. The bobbins were in place and occasionally they flicked as fish moved to and fro, backwards and forwards across the

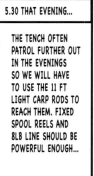

swim. We'd decided to bait very heavily with maggots, far more intensively than Mr. Crabtree would ever have done. In fact, between around eight and eleven o'clock we had catapulted in well over twelve pints of reds. Such a thing, I suspect, would have had Mr. Crabtree grinding on his pipe stem. However, the ruse worked. More and more Crabtree-like tench bubbles began to rise to the surface. More and more fatly amber tench began to roll in front of us. This traditional scene was being set in a distinctly modern way.

My float first went down around 10.45 in the morning, which, in itself, is distinctly un-Crabtree. Most tench fishing fifty or sixty years back was deemed to be past its prime once the sun was well up. In the deeper waters of the gravel pit, you don't have to be such an early bird as this first, fine fish proved. I didn't weigh it – it was perhaps seven pounds and a bit – just a few ounces short of the record back in Mr. Crabtree's day. Yes, sometimes, I have to pinch myself.

From then on, however, all the action was Sam's. Those initial flicks and bumps on the bobbins and the rod tip began to intensify. Soon, as the morning veered towards lunchtime, the bite indicators began singing merrily. Sam had an extraordinary session. In two hectic hours or so, he broke his personal best three, then four times and his run to the tenching moon culminated in one of the most glorious female tench it's been my privilege to witness. Nine pounds of exquisite fish glory had both man and boy gawping. Mr. Crabtree taught that the size of a fish is absolutely not the first priority and Bernard himself developed a real distaste for the naked ambition of specimen hunting. Yes, success should never be determined by size but there was something about that tench that simply glowed. It was as good a moment as I've ever experienced in my tenching career, certainly since that morning at Holkham Lake half a century ago.

What are the big lessons that we have learnt about tench fishing in the sixty years since Mr. Crabtree set down his and Peter's stools?

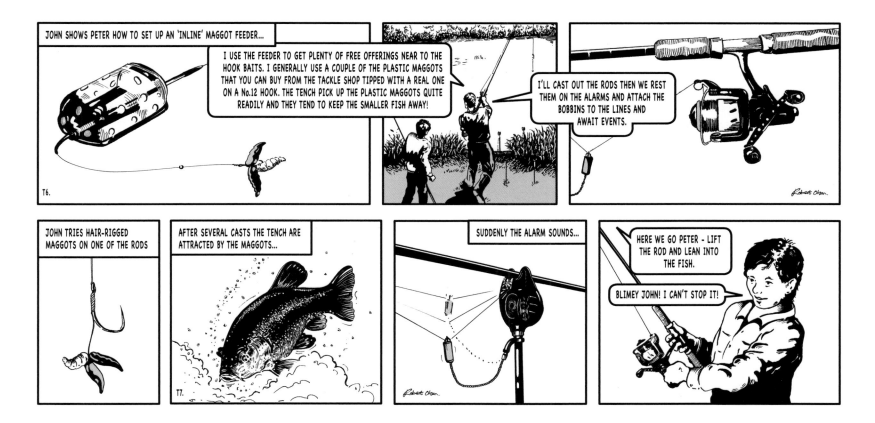

Well, first, we know that tench can still be caught traditionally, close in using a float as an indicator. The centrepin reel is still the perfect tool for the job but we'd probably now choose a waggler float and take great care with our bait presentation. Maggots, worms and bread in all its various forms still catch tench as they did for Peter but we'd add sweetcorn to the list now, a bait only discovered twenty years after Mr. Crabtree was created. The fishing that Mr. Crabtree and Peter so enjoyed is still the most exciting form of tench fishing that there is and, thankfully, is the most straightforward.

But we know, today, that many big tench exist at range, often in shoals. This is why we will use ledger rigs of one sort or another. The method feeder is a modern but fairly straightforward approach. There's nothing magic, either, in using an inline feeder technique, probably with maggots. Both these tactics open up your tench fishing and probably will result in bigger bags of fish overall. And some of the very big tench today come on mini-carp techniques, using small boilies with self-

hooking rigs at range. Again, there is nothing complex here but some of the intimacy of traditional tenching is lost.

Gravel pits have, to a large degree, taken over from traditional estate lakes and ponds and location is more difficult. However, sighting fish is still essential so look for them rolling on the surface. The bars and plateaux in gravel pits are always good tench-holding spots but the gulleys, especially close in, attract fish, too. Be aware on gravel pits that tench are highly nomadic and will often move from one day to the next, so be

prepared to sacrifice that favourite swim if you feel the fish have deserted it.

One bonus about gravel pits is that the tench aren't quite as addicted to early morning feeding as they are in shallower estate lakes. Some of the best tench fishing actually comes today between eight a.m. and one or two p.m.

Weather, however, is vital. Tench do not like a falling barometer, cold winds and heavy rain. If the pressure is steady and rising and the air temperature warm for several days, then the tench can really begin to feed. Until you are confident on gravel pits, it makes sense to fish smaller, more densely stocked waters for tench. The size of the fish you catch is not important. What is vital is the knowledge of the species that you're building up.

The last few years have been very kind to my tench fishing and I've caught an extraordinary number of fish over the nine pound mark, an achievement I would have thought quite impossible back in my early Crabtree days when the record was just over seven pounds. However, in spite of all these successes, my greatest Mr. Crabtree moments have always taken place on estate lakes full of tench. It's on the estate lake that the fatly amber tench is in her most glorious habitat.

Of all the estate lakes, Bayfield Lake in Norfolk will always be the home of my happiest memories. There, you could watch the tench graze the glistening sandy shallows as the summer sun clambered in the sky. The lake, towards its dam end, is cloaked in the most glorious woodland, providing the perfect backdrop to the most perfect tench.

We used to catch them, Crabtree-like, underneath floats. Floats were always the way at Bayfield and they'd weave and curtsey and they'd dip and dive and the beautiful fish would show their flanks in the crystal clear, sunlit waters as they fought. There has never been anything like Bayfield tenching for me.

Perhaps you've noticed the past tense throughout. Bayfield tench are no more. After living there for so long, they have been annihilated by marauding otters. All of them. There's not a fish of any species left in the lake. Everything has gone. And as a result, there are now no kingfishers, grebes or herons. Most of the wildfowl have been eaten, too. Bayfield is a graveyard.

This book should be a celebration of Mr. Crabtree, a reawakening of all the joys that he gave us. However, Bayfield is a reminder that we can never take the health of our waters for granted, that we should enjoy every moment that we spend in our aquatic wonderland.

All our waters are precious because of their fragility, and their angling fortunes ebb and flow in tune with every other aspect of the natural world.

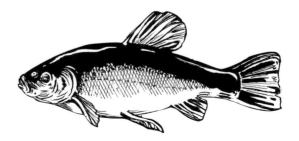

*Illustration by Bernard Venables from*
*Mr. Crabtree Goes Fishing.*

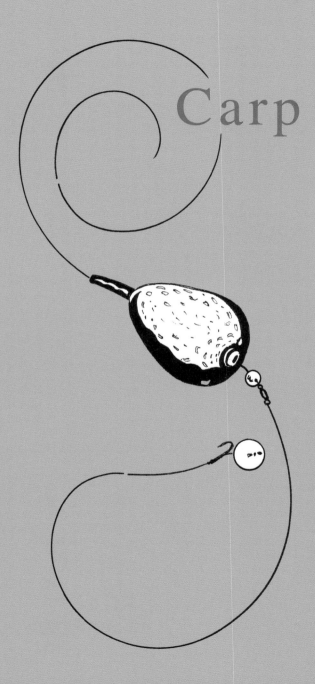

# Carp

"Of all the fish of the Summer the Carp is unrivalled. No other can give such sport. But not all fishermen are equal to the test of it, for he who fishes for Carp must be ready to do so with the greatest devotion."

*Bernard Venables M.B.E. - Mr. Crabtree Goes Fishing.*

If, magically, Mr. Crabtree could be brought to flesh and blood life sixty or more years after his creation as a cartoon, his fishing results would be interesting to observe. I guess he'd catch as many river roach on the float as anyone alive today. Probably far more. In Mr. Crabtree's day, river roaching was an art form of huge proportions and a lot of the skills are, today, sadly buried and lost. They are kept alive in only small, hushed circles of anglers around the country and the reappearance of Mr. Crabtree would be like a Messiah returning.

Mr. Crabtree would still catch large numbers of pike, without doubt. He evidently knew exactly how to get the best out of both bait and lure methods and though things have progressed in both areas, he'd quickly cotton on to the changes. Where he would have to sharpen up his act considerably is in the care and conservation of the species. If he appeared on a water today with a gaff and a gag and then carted the corpse off to Mrs. Crabtree's kitchen, he'd likely find himself strung up from the nearest tree.

TEN MINUTES LATER...

LOOK PETER, KEEP AS STILL AS YOU CAN - SEE THOSE REEDS NUDGING? A SURE SIGN THAT CARP ARE INVESTIGATING THE MARGINS.

CP2.

I'LL RUN AND GET THE ROD JOHN!

NO, PETER! THAT IS SURE TO PANIC THEM. I'LL FLICK IN A HALF A DOZEN HALIBUT PELLETS, ONE AT A TIME, SO AS NOT TO SPOOK THEM AND WE'LL SNEAK BACK IN HALF AN HOUR TO SEE IF THEY ARE STILL HERE.

Robert Olsen.

HALF WAY AROUND THE LAKE...

THERE PETER! LOOK AT THAT COLOURED WATER AND THOSE BUBBLES BY THE MARGINAL LILY PADS! CARP GRUBBING AROUND IN THE SILT FOR SURE.

I'LL FLICK A FEW PELLETS HERE TOO PETER - I THINK WE'VE SEEN ENOUGH TO NIP BACK AND SET UP THE ROD.

CP3.

BACK BY THEIR TACKLE JOHN SETS UP A LIGHT CARP ROD WHILST PETER ASSEMBLES THE NET AND THEN WATCHES AS JOHN SHOWS HIM HOW TO ASSEMBLE THE REMAINDER OF TACKLE THAT HE FEELS WILL GIVE THEM THEIR BEST CHANCE...

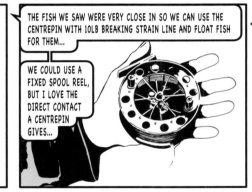

THE FISH WE SAW WERE VERY CLOSE IN SO WE CAN USE THE CENTREPIN WITH 10LB BREAKING STRAIN LINE AND FLOAT FISH FOR THEM...

WE COULD USE A FIXED SPOOL REEL, BUT I LOVE THE DIRECT CONTACT A CENTREPIN GIVES...

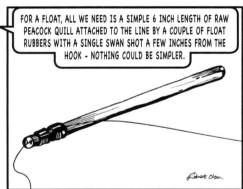

FOR A FLOAT, ALL WE NEED IS A SIMPLE 6 INCH LENGTH OF RAW PEACOCK QUILL ATTACHED TO THE LINE BY A COUPLE OF FLOAT RUBBERS WITH A SINGLE SWAN SHOT A FEW INCHES FROM THE HOOK - NOTHING COULD BE SIMPLER.

Robert Olsen.

On some of the more difficult, larger tench waters, Mr. Crabtree would be struggling in the twenty-first century. He'd still manage to catch tench, though, on smaller, prolific waters using his tactics from the 1940s. His bream fishing, too, he would find more than capable of adapting itself to today's conditions. I think Mr. Crabtree would prove himself to be a pretty mean barbel angler as well. I love his trotting technique, feeding the stream heavily with maggots as he fishes. It's a method that I've used to huge effect on many rivers and barbel never seem to tire of a stream of little white grubs. Mr. Crabtree, though, might find it advisable to call them maggots rather than 'gentles' in these less than sophisticated times. I'd hate to think of him being mocked in the modern tackle shop.

It's very evident that Mr. Crabtree was at home on the river and understood all the nuances and sophistications of moving water. I'm not sure that Mr. Crabtree's Wallis casting techniques stand up to extreme scrutiny, though today he'd probably use the fixed spool reel to achieve big casting distances. Killing a six

THE PELLETS WE FLICKED IN ARE SURE TO HAVE INTERESTED THE CARP WE SAW SO WE'LL THREAD A SINGLE PELLET ON TO A HAIR RIG AND TRY OUR LUCK...

BACK BY THE REEDS...

NOW PETER - IT'S VERY IMPORTANT THAT WE TAKE OUR TIME AND KEEP OUT OF SIGHT - CARP ARE VERY SUSPICIOUS FISH - WE ONLY HAVE ONE CHANCE.

NOW, I'LL PEEL A LITTLE LINE OFF THE REEL AND SWING THE TACKLE TOWARDS THE REEDS, THEN WE'LL CROUCH DOWN BEHIND THE REEDS AND WAIT...

ONCE IN POSITION...

THERE WE ARE - TAKE THE ROD PETER, REST IT ON THE REEDS TO STEADY IT, AND GENTLY TIGHTEN THE LINE SO THE FLOAT COCKS AGAINST THE SINGLE SWANSHOT RESTING ON THE BOTTOM.

pound chub to set up in a glass case would also raise eyebrows and I'd advise Mr. Crabtree to slip all chub back just as soon as possible. I'd hate Peter to observe an ugly incident on the river bank.

Mr. Crabtree was absolutely no slouch with rudd and definitely not so with perch. In fact, he'd adore the perch fishing of today now the species is back in numbers in so many waters, achieving really spectacular sizes to boot. There's absolutely nothing wrong with anything that Mr. Crabtree preaches about either species back in the late 1940s and I'd back him to hold his own today against anyone.

However, when it comes to the carp, I guess Mr. Crabtree would have to put out his pipe, sit down and begin all over again. The ten pounder in the cartoon would never have materialised either then or now in reality. He and Peter would have trudged home fishless from one carp session after another. We nearly all did in the middle years of the last century. That's how carp fishing was. At least, nearly always.

Today, of course, the carp is arguably the country's most popular fish. In the 1940s, Bernard devoted a mere three pages to the fish's capture. Carp were just not on the agenda for most anglers. Firstly, there were far fewer of them. To try and find a carp water then was always an uphill task. And if you did stumble on a water where carp were resident, the common belief was that they were pretty well uncatchable. I learnt this myself on a summer's day in 1960, visiting a lake in Greater Manchester with my own Mr. Crabtree, Ron, a local builder.

In the blazing heat, I tired a little of catching the small roach and kept casting envious eyes at a distant lily bed where half a dozen carp were lazily spending the afternoon. Why, oh why, can we not catch those, I asked Ron on an almost minute by minute basis. He replied firmly that, firstly, the carp would refuse to bite. And second, he added that if one did bite, it might just as well not have done because we would lose it anyway.

In the end, my pestering paid off and Ron took his strongest rod from the back of his three-wheeler and set it up with line strong enough to hang a conger eel. We rustled up a loaf of bread, pulled off a corner of crust and Ron cast it thirty or forty yards into the middle of the lilies. The afternoon wore on until, eventually, a head appeared, the lips engulfed the bread and the line streamed out. Ron leapt up, struck and the line parted like the proverbial pistol shot. The lilies exploded and all the carp fled towards the setting sun. Ron shrugged, turned to me and said simply, told you so. You don't bother with carp.

But that one failure spurred me on as all failures should.

By the early '60s, I'd found a lock pool on a canal, reputed to hold carp up to the dizzy size of twelve or even fifteen pounds. Faced with such a paradise on earth, I returned to Mr. Crabtree. Following instructions, I par-boiled a couple of pounds of potatoes, cycled to the lock pool in question and deposited them in the crystal clear water, close to a sunken barge. Day after day, I visited the pool to observe results. The potatoes remained there throughout the entire summer holidays. Not as much as a piece of skin was nibbled. That was fifty years ago and I guess those

potatoes are still there, fossilised, to this day.

I once wrote an article asking if anybody anywhere had caught a carp on a par-boiled potato. I did receive one or two irate responses from old-time-traditionalists who swore blind that the potato would always win through. However, ninety-five percent of communications agreed with me: par-boiled potatoes must be without doubt the most hopeless carp bait that was ever dreamed up. Throughout the 1960s my carping mates and I drowned whole fieldfuls of the things without a single carp, or run come to that, to my name. That's why for so long, I reverted to the floating crust, the method that Ron had taught me and a method, too, that Bernard writes about in Mr. Crabtree. I don't think Bernard quite understood the technique perfectly. For example, he talks about the method working on a windy day... it will but give me a flat calm any time! Thank you, though, Bernard and Ron alike: floating crust served me well both then, now and throughout my carping life.

My first ever carp came on floating crust, at a hideously commercialised local lake in Greater Manchester, on a Sunday night when the shadows had fallen and the day-trippers had largely headed for home. I was the last on the lake, taking a great risk of a clout and a kick up the backside from the owner when the fish took. A dark, rhino-back appeared, the slurp was historic and the line slithered out. A five pound common carp was, then, just about the greatest thing that had ever happened to me.

The carping revolution that would have totally baffled Mr. Crabtree, started in the 1970s and gathered pace through the 1980s and 1990s. The lessons learnt during those dynamic years changed the face of carp fishing in every single conceivable way. Absolutely nothing that Mr. Crabtree taught Peter remains intact. In the field of carp fishing, Mr. Crabtree has been completely obliterated.

We could say that small, par-boiled potatoes look a little like pale, similar-sized boilies but, really, we're clutching at straws. The science of boilies is nothing remotely like that most basic recipe of simmering a few potatoes in boiling water. And as for rigs,

Mr. Crabtree would never even have dreamt of fishing a bait on a hair, not even attached to the hook. I remember taking an old friend very much of the Crabtree era carp fishing in the late 1970s. When I set up his hair-rigged boilie he looked at me as though I should be institutionalised. When I added the fixed lead, self-hooking rig, he just knew I was totally insane. And that was in the early years of modern carp fishing. What he or Mr. Crabtree would make of snowman rigs, z-rigs, helicopter rigs and the rest, I just cannot begin to imagine.

Mr. Crabtree and Peter sit on their stools with their rod in the crook of a branch taken from the nearest tree. Their line is coiled on brown paper and that's their carp fishing. A par-boiled potato at one end and a hopeful incompetent at the other! There's not a bivvy or a bed chair or an electronic bite alarm in sight. There's no mention of spods or bait runners and Mr. Crabtree's landing net looks as though it would buckle under the weight of even an average-sized carp in the new century.

For a long while, I was totally bewitched by this new wave of carp fishing. From the mid 1970s to the mid 1990s I was as keen as any carp angler could be. It was during this period that I co-wrote Carp – the Quest for the Queen, still one of the better selling carp books of the last century and one often mentioned in despatches today. For a few years, I had a proud place in the carp record books of Norfolk with three fish over thirty pounds, one an absolute giant then of thirty-four pounds plus. I was even invited to talk at carp conferences and knew the likes of carping giants like Kevin Clifford, Rod Hutchinson, Chris Yates, Kevin Nash, Ritchie Macdonald and the rest of the species heroes. Today, I am Fishery Director at a modern, high-level carp lake. I marvel at what the boys are doing there sixty years after Crabtree. Their watercraft is extraordinary, and Bernard would approve of that. Their understanding of weather fluctuations is top-notch. Their preparation is mind-bogglingly effective. Their skills in action are complete. They can put a lead and a boily on a sixpence at a hundred and fifty yards range. It's common,

in some quarters to knock the modern carp angler but he is an extraordinary creation, the result of forty years carping development. In that short time, we've gone from Crabtree's potato to almost indescribable levels of sophistication.

Personally I dropped off this bandwagon some fifteen or so years ago. Time became too tight for me to spend a lifetime in a bivvy, camping by a carp lake. Because of this, I began to revert more and more to the traditional methods. They might not have been methods that Mr. Crabtree taught Peter, but they were getting close. Today, when I do go carp fishing, I like, still, to take them off the top. I think I know a lot now about surface fishing. The small, scented, floating boilies and pellets have made life considerably easier than the days when the only option was a piece of floating bread. Floating bread, though, can still win through.

If I'm not taking carp off the top, then I still enjoy pursuing them with a float over a bed of bait. I like to get them in close, where I can see their reaction to everything happening

around them. I love to see the bubbles as they work. I thrill at seeing the flank of a carp upending, going down to the bed where I know my bait is lying. I love warm days, when the lake is still and it's possible to stalk fish, watching them feed in the shallows, perhaps, where I can trick them with a lob or a bunch of small red worms. Perhaps I'll even sprinkle a rain of 'gentles' around them and entice them to my net that way.

It's interesting that Mr. Crabtree takes Peter along carp fishing merely as an observer. I feel in this Bernard Venables was absolutely correct. There's a trend these days for children to start off with carp as a beginner fish. This, I'm convinced, is not the way to teach a child, if he's going to be an angler for life. Carp are great and they are desirable but a youngster has to work his way up to the exalted level of fishing that they pose. If you start a child with fish of twenty or thirty pounds then there are not many other species that he can lock into in the future.

Happily, there's still a lot of Crabtree in carp fishing today. A couple of years back, I was sitting tench fishing on a carp lake, my bottom on the bankside. One of the older members of the club came up and asked politely if I could just move a few inches. It seemed that I was sitting on the most toothsome bed of water mint anywhere around the water. He picked a few sprigs and took them away to flavour his boiling Jersey Royals, he said. And by the way, those Jersey Royals were to accompany his sausage supper rather than to be used as bait!

My Mr. Crabtree carp cherished moments are very special ones. I could talk about the Boathouse Lake, a water I worshipped in the 80s and 90s. Its peaks for me were early mornings, stalking carp up in the shallows towards the hall where they would forage for their breakfast. It would be possible to get close to the feeding giants, to watch their backs break the surface, their tails wave clear in the milky morning light. There a sprinkling of maggots would often bring their downfall with a bunch of three or four on a small, strong hook layed on under a Crabtree-type quill. Once hooked, because of the shallow water, those carp, often nudging thirty pounds or just over, would

rampage off with such speed that even I would be wide-eyed as Peter. The adrenaline of those moments buzzes within me still.

Or I could talk about my own English forty pounder taken off the top, on floating crust, just as Mr. Crabtree prescribed. It was a wonderful day, a typical English summer's day when the wood pigeons sang and the lake was cradled in the warmth of the sun. My modern baits and rigs had lain unmolested since the very early hours, since just before dawn and not a bleep had registered on the indicators. However, just after lunch, the

leviathan carp appeared, wallowing in an arm of the lake where the water was thickly filmed with the flotsam and jetsam of the day. He came to my crust – he obviously smelt it instantly. He nosed it. He sniffed it. And then he engulfed it. Apart from its impossibly large size, that scene was as Crabtree as you like.

Fishing in the Footsteps of Mr. Crabtree, though, has to be authentic above all, and my very best Crabtree moment really has to be this. Happily, it took place when filming the first series of programmes. Michael is ten years old and his carping

THE CARP ROCKETS OFF AND FIGHTS LONG AND HARD BUT, WITH JOHN'S STEADY ADVICE, PETER EVENTUALLY STEERS WHAT LOOKS LIKE A HUGE FISH TOWARDS THE WAITING NET.

experience was correspondingly limited. I took him, as my Peter for the two days, to a wonderful, private lake where the carp are fat and gorgeous. He landed two magnificent fish. One was a mirror carp of sixteen pounds and another, unbelievably, a common of just over twenty-two. In truth, on reflection, these fish really were too big for a wee one of such a tender age. He played the fish well, though, and was obviously happy with them. Who wouldn't be? If I'd ever thought of catching fish of such sizes at his age, I would have skipped to the moon. There was something dazed, though, about Michael's reaction to all this. I sensed it was all a little too much.

Then, I took him to Lily Lake. It's a small water this, not quite as beautiful but heavily stocked with nice-sized fish of between five and twelve pounds. The glory of Lily Lake is that these fellows like to feed off the top. This is what turned Michael on and what made him the most bubbling of Peters.

On a dreary, drizzly afternoon, we found the carp up an arm of the lake, feeding hard under the overhanging trees and along the reedy margins. We put in the dog biscuits and, one by one, the carp began to sniff the water and come up to feed. This is what Michael realised Crabtree carp fishing is all about. His eyes stood out like chapel hat pegs. His attention was riveted. The spell these carp cast was unbreakable. A fish came to his biscuit. The line tightened. He struck and he missed and the water boiled in a volcano of anger. He tried to re-bait, his hands literally shaking with excitement. I took over but I noticed my fingers were equally unreliable. Between us we got a bait back in the water and managed an eight pound common. This was the Peter excitement the film crew wanted to witness. This was the Peter smile I'd been waiting for. This was Michael's own achievement. This is the legacy of Mr. Crabtree.

# Fish Safety

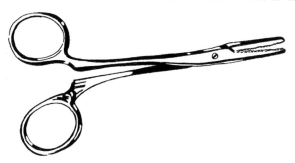

In Mr. Crabtree's day, fish were not harmed unless killed cleanly for the table, but their care and conservation were at an early stage. Today, there are far more anglers and this means that the fish that we catch must be looked after with much more consideration.

Mr. Crabtree talks about keep nets. In those days, these were miserable, tiny, damagingly knotted affairs which did the fish a heap of no good. Apart from matches, may I suggest that a keep net is a thing of the past?

Nor does Mr. Crabtree mention unhooking mats, which are now obligatory on very many fisheries and universally accepted as part of good fishing practice. These are soft, padded mats which should be well wetted and provide a soft, secure base upon which to lay a fish ready for unhooking. Keep the fish well wetted on the mat as well, especially in the summer.

Unhooking tools have changed considerably. When piking, Mr. Crabtree used a gaff, an ugly hook, to insert under the pike's chin instead of a landing net. These are relics of a distant age as are gags, metal springs that force the pike's mouth wide open. Today, we have properly designed pliers for unhooking pike.

We realise today that it's important to get the fish back into the water fast. Make sure your unhooking techniques are swift and effective and if you want to weigh and photograph a fish, if it is a special trophy, do this with the minimum of fuss and time.

**Let's remember the three big rules.**

**One** – always handle fish with wet hands. That layer of slime that surrounds them is there for good purpose, protecting them against every water bourne danger.

**Two** – if you can unhook a fish in the margins by flicking the hook out with forceps, do so. It's really important to keep fish in their natural habitat if at all possible.

**Three** – always use either barbless or micro-barbed hooks if at all possible.

Finally, remember that as an angler you are the eyes of the fishery. Always be alert for any poaching or especially pollution incidents. Do not ever get involved yourself but always be ready to phone the Environment Agency hotline to report incidents. **(0800 807060)**

# Carp Rigs & Methods

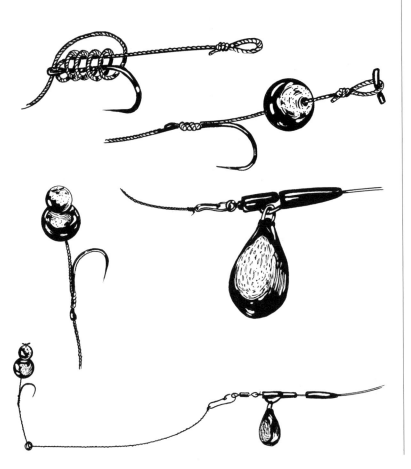

The pursuit of carp has seen the most dramatic of changes from the days when Mr. Crabtree was using par-boiled potatoes and meat paste. Mr. Crabtree was certainly no slouch, he was using the best methods, rigs, and baits of the time, but carping, more than any other area of fishing, has been transformed in the decades since then.

Don't be too intimidated by the immense, apparent complexity of carp rigs and methods that are out there in the carp fishing media today. A lot of the more complex approaches have very specialised windows of opportunity and you can safely embark on your carp fishing career using really quite simple rigs.

There's a lot about the so-called science of carp fishing today that is confusing in the extreme. Try to think clearly and, above all, understand what your own set-up is trying to achieve. Of paramount importance is the safety of your rigs. You never want to use a line that is too fragile for the fish or for the water that you are fishing. You must not run risks of breakages. If the worst should happen, the rig that you have lost to the fish must be a safe one and must come free so that the carp is never tethered.

We are going to look at some of the ideas that have most impacted and shaped modern carp fishing and that also form the basis of many of the more advanced set ups used. Most of these are no longer exclusive to carpers and are employed by anglers targeting a variety of species.

## The Boilie

First dreamed up in the 1970s by Fred Wilton, the boilie is now one of the most commonly used carp baits. Boilies come in a dizzying array of colours, flavours, sizes and types, but essentially they are boiled paste fishing baits, usually combining a variety of fishmeals, milk proteins and bird foods, mixed with eggs as a binding agent and then boiled to form hardish, spherical baits.

The sky really is the limit when it comes to flavour and attractors and I have seen many weird and wonderful additions. A boilie can last a long time out in the water, and its hardened exterior means that smaller fish can't take the hookbait or whittle it down before a carp comes along.

## The Hair Rig

The hair rig is a very clever piece of fishing improvisation that allows us to present baits without them sitting directly on the hook, thereby improving efficiency. Initially associated with boilies, the hair rig works just as effectively with many other baits. Devised and developed by some of the most legendary anglers of the 1970s this rig really did revolutionise carp fishing and continues to be one of the most significant of angling inventions. By allowing the boilie to sit off the back of the hook we create a situation whereby the bait will behave more naturally in the water and can achieve fantastic hook holds.

## The Knotless Knot

There are several ways to present the bait and at first the originators used light braid, dental floss or actual hair tied to the bend in the hook. These days the most common method is to tie the knotless knot, which is a great way to secure your hook to your hook-length.

## The Bolt Rig

The bolt rig was first developed using a fixed weight on the line. The thinking behind it was that a fish would pick up the bait, feel the weight and 'bolt', thereby hooking itself securely. Nowadays a far safer type of bolt rig is most often used – The Safety Bolt Rig using the safety bead first invented and produced by Kevin Nash. The main principle behind this rig is that the lead, whilst still performing a bolt effect, can be ejected, making it very safe. It's also a good way to present a bait and is reasonably tangle proof.

## Pop-up rigs

Pop-up rigs enable us to present our bait just off the lake or river bottom, something that is very useful when positioning the bait above any weed or general detritus that could mask a bottom bait. There are a variety of options based around this theme, ranging from critically balancing your baits to fool a wary carp, to how far off the bottom you might want to present your bait. More recently this has led to the development of the highly effective zig-rig where the bait can be presented at any depth. Sometimes it gives us the opportunity just to do something a little bit different. Carp anglers will often deploy a bright and highly flavoured bait to interest and lure a curious carp.

## The Method

Groundbait has always been used in one way or another in fishing, harking back way before even Mr. Crabtree's day. The Method takes a mixture of groundbait and particles moulded around a specially designed weight or a cage feeder. It enables a bed of bait to be placed on the bottom with your hookbait in or very near to it. A cunning way to present your hookbait amongst your free offerings, the Method provides accurate baiting, with the additional benefits of being tangle proof and ideal when fishing on a variety of bottom conditions and in weed.

## PVA Bags

A favourite method for anglers today is the use of PVA bags. The inclusion of this water soluble material as a staple in the tackle boxes of most carp anglers is testament to its efficacy in introducing a parcel of bait, whether it be pellets, particles, maggots or crushed up boilies, very close to your hookbait. A simple and effective method, it is resistant to tangles and lends itself to a long cast, providing the potential to fool a wary fish not expecting to come across a tasty bed of bait right out in the middle of the lake.

*Illustration by Bernard Venables from*
*Mr. Crabtree Goes Fishing.*

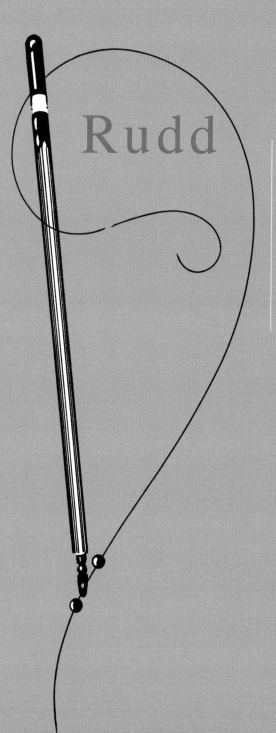

# Rudd

"It is suffused all over with a shine of gold. Its eye is more red than the eye of the Roach. And all its fins are red... but beyond this the Rudd is a bulkier fish, a fine thick-shouldered solid fish. It is indeed very handsome."

*Bernard Venables M.B.E. - Mr. Crabtree Goes Fishing.*

Bernard Venables' view of the future could be bleak if you read deeper into the words accompanying the Crabtree cartoons. He was worried about pollution, abstraction, dredging, poor river management and the future of many fish species. Today, the rudd is perhaps the fish that has found the going the toughest of all. Many of their pits and ponds have disappeared under development. Many populations have been pressured out of existence by the spread of stocked carp. And, in many places, they have hybridised with roach and bream, losing that purity that makes them so startlingly beautiful.

It's not all bad news and there are places where you can still hunt rudd and marvel at what are the most awesome of our freshwater beauties. Bernard called them handsome but I would go further. In 1958, I saw my first rudd and I fell in love that moment. It was late in the summer holidays – one advantage of keeping a fishing diary since the age of six is that you can remember small things with startling clarity. It was a burningly hot day and I was at Poynton Pool, deep in Cheshire, when a

RIGHT PETER, LET'S SEE IF WE CAN CATCH ONE OF OUR MOST BEAUTIFUL FISH - A RUDD.

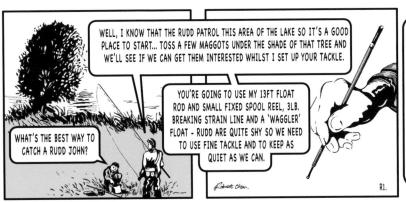

WELL, I KNOW THAT THE RUDD PATROL THIS AREA OF THE LAKE SO IT'S A GOOD PLACE TO START... TOSS A FEW MAGGOTS UNDER THE SHADE OF THAT TREE AND WE'LL SEE IF WE CAN GET THEM INTERESTED WHILST I SET UP YOUR TACKLE.

WHAT'S THE BEST WAY TO CATCH A RUDD JOHN?

YOU'RE GOING TO USE MY 13FT FLOAT ROD AND SMALL FIXED SPOOL REEL, 3LB. BREAKING STRAIN LINE AND A 'WAGGLER' FLOAT - RUDD ARE QUITE SHY SO WE NEED TO USE FINE TACKLE AND TO KEEP AS QUIET AS WE CAN.

Robert Olsen.                R1.

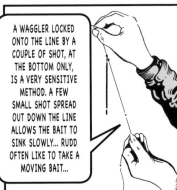

A WAGGLER LOCKED ONTO THE LINE BY A COUPLE OF SHOT, AT THE BOTTOM ONLY, IS A VERY SENSITIVE METHOD. A FEW SMALL SHOT SPREAD OUT DOWN THE LINE ALLOWS THE BAIT TO SINK SLOWLY... RUDD OFTEN LIKE TO TAKE A MOVING BAIT...

fellow angler landed the fish. Its golden scales just glowed in the sunlight and its scarlet fins were a colour I'd never seen before. Its deep, dazzling body made it an almost impossible fish for me to take in. I've been in thrall now for fifty-odd years.

If you can find your rudd, if you are quiet, they're not difficult to catch. Or at least the first one or two are not, before the shoal grows uneasy and fades away into the farther regions of the pool. Rudd are uniquely skittish. They're like

small, highly-coloured birds that flit this way and that in their tightly-controlled flocks. I've been eternally lucky to watch them in crystal waters, playing around lilies and among the stems of reeds and bulrushes. Their alertness is frightening, their speed electrifying. They are always on the fin, explosions of red and gold.

I like small, secluded waters for my rudd fishing. Mr. Crabtree mentions larger ones like Heigham Sound on the Norfolk Broads but even here you can locate rudd in the bays and feel you are in a tight, intimate swim with your fish. My own great rudd water

WHAT A LOVELY GOLDEN COLOUR!

HOLD HER UP OVER THE WATER PETER AND I'LL TAKE A QUICK PHOTOGRAPH, THEN WE CAN RELEASE HER SAFELY.

PETER FISHES ON FOR AN HOUR BUT ONLY CATCHES TWO MORE SMALLER RUDD BEFORE THE SPORT DRIES UP.

JUST AS THEY THINK THEY HAVE HAD THE BEST OF THE DAY, JOHN SPOTS SOME ACTIVITY ON THE SURFACE AT THE OTHER SIDE OF THE LAKE.

LOOK PETER! SEE THAT DISTURBANCE BY THOSE REEDS? A GROUP OF RUDD ARE CRUISING NEAR THE TOP. LET'S SNEAK AROUND WITH THE ROD AND NET AND SEE IF WE CAN TEMPT ONE TO TAKE A BAIT OFF THE SURFACE.

ONCE IN POSITION...

I'LL TOSS IN A FEW CUBES OF BREAD CRUST AND SEE WHAT HAPPENS.

of the present is tiny. I guess it's barely an acre and it lies nestled in a deep scoop of land, surrounded by whispering trees and an almost impenetrable guard of bulrushes. Throughout the spring, summer and well into autumn, this little rudd oasis is simply festooned with weed and you are searching for your fish in the tiniest pockets amongst it.

Perhaps because the water is so shrouded, it's almost impossible to tell exactly what swims within. Herein lies one of the charms of the place: I've caught rudd to over a pound and a half and plenty between twelve and sixteen ounces but there's always this intoxicating feeling that bigger fish lie just out of reach. If you're quiet, particularly at dawn, you will pick up on huge swirls, swirls certainly larger than a mere pounder could conceivably produce. Sometimes, too, a piece of crust will disappear in thick weed, inside a mouth that seems impossibly large for any fish less than two or even three pounds. You might ask why I don't fish the lake in the winter when the weed is gone and the rudd would, almost surely, be easier to catch. I

should. I don't know what stops me. Perhaps it's some slavish observance to Mr. Crabtree's doctrine that rudd are a fish of the warm months. Or perhaps by then I've got my pike hat on or my river roach or my chub, or whatever fish it is that takes me away from this wondrously beautiful little place.

I think there is this to my thinking as well. Possibly, if I really did know the full extent of the rudd in my little lake, might I be disappointed? Do I feed on the dreams of the monster? Do I simply, deep down, fear that the rudd might peter out not much above that pound and a half mark and my monsters are simply massive in my mind? Of course, this shouldn't matter and it doesn't. A rudd of a pound or a pound and a half is simply exquisite. It's one of those fish that makes your heart sing, making you long for the days when you were still a Crabtree kid.

Mr. Crabtree, as ever, got it right when he said you pursue rudd simply. I like to fish a waggler with a weight around the bottom of the float so the bait sinks slowly and naturally down

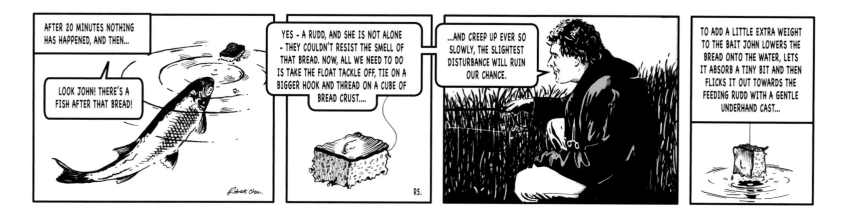

AFTER 20 MINUTES NOTHING HAS HAPPENED, AND THEN...

LOOK JOHN! THERE'S A FISH AFTER THAT BREAD!

YES - A RUDD, AND SHE IS NOT ALONE - THEY COULDN'T RESIST THE SMELL OF THAT BREAD. NOW, ALL WE NEED TO DO IS TAKE THE FLOAT TACKLE OFF, TIE ON A BIGGER HOOK AND THREAD ON A CUBE OF BREAD CRUST....

...AND CREEP UP EVER SO SLOWLY, THE SLIGHTEST DISTURBANCE WILL RUIN OUR CHANCE.

TO ADD A LITTLE EXTRA WEIGHT TO THE BAIT JOHN LOWERS THE BREAD ONTO THE WATER, LETS IT ABSORB A TINY BIT AND THEN FLICKS IT OUT TOWARDS THE FEEDING RUDD WITH A GENTLE UNDERHAND CAST...

through the water column. Maggots are my favourite bait for this. Two on a size 16 hook are about right and you scatter loose maggot in like gently freckling rain around the float. Flake is pretty well equally as good and you catapult a snowstorm of pinched, wetted mash regularly around that red-top float. Soon you will see fish flashing, even coming to the surface to take pieces of crust that don't quite sink. If the fish are big, this is one of the most exciting moments in freshwater fishing.

Best of all, I like my rudd fishing on a summer or early autumn dusk after a warm, still day. This is the time to see big rudd feeding on the surface, picking off hatching midges and moths struggling in the surface film. The lights of the sky absolutely mirror the colours of the fish and the deeper the reds and golds become, the harder the rudd feed.

Again, keep your fishing Crabtree simple. A tiny float, perhaps a little crow quill, hook and flake pressed just tight enough to sink ever so slowly is all the kit you need for the biggest of fish. Look for them where the debris of the day has

settled on the surface. See the rudd tenting up the skim of nature's detritus that has gathered to a glutinous skin by the evening time. Or find the rudd in the reeds themselves and watch the stems quivering as the fish push through.

There's an urgency to catch a last fish before the light finally extinguishes and you walk back through the wood. Any rudd will do but a pounder, or more, would be spectacular on such a night. Do take care. Rudd fight above their weight, far harder than their cousin the roach, and you will need a four pound line to hold the fish from the reeds and branches fallen from the trees. Now comes that heavy swirl at your flake that hangs just underneath the surface and the line slithers tight. Wait until every last wrinkle has been ironed out straight and lift into your rudd. It's a pound and a half and it disappears back with showering droplets of gold.

Arguably, the red-hot rudd fishing of the present day is to be found in the drains of Fenland and I would suggest Ely is as good a place as any to begin. Of course, you'll have to explore.

These long, seemingly featureless waterways crisscross for miles over endless acres of flat, agricultural land. I guess finding the big rudd that are certainly present there is very much needle in haystack stuff and, for that reason I've tended to shy away. Perhaps, if someone would gift me an unexpectedly free week then I'd make my way those sixty or seventy miles west from my present cottage and begin my exploration for those Fenland giants.

Finally, Mr. Crabtree rightly talks about catching rudd on fly and they are hugely susceptible to this method. On Mr. Crabtree's suggestion I've picked them up here and there throughout the years on small, dry flies... I remember a particularly splendid specimen caught from the delta of the Ural River in Kazakhstan. It was a fish so splendid from a place so wonderful that I always dream of going back.

However, my best fly-caught rudd fell for something a little bit different. It was dawn - always a sensational time for the species - and I was stalking a shoal of big fish on a secluded estate lake. I'd found them in the shallows under the trees where they were swirling heavily for falling insects. As the sun rose over the hill, as the mists streamed off and the light entered the water, I realised I was in pursuit of ten or perhaps twelve rudd, all of two and a half pounds or over. This is the moment when your hands begin to shake, when the sweat forms on your brow.

I had with me a simple five weight fly outfit, a few dries and a box of nymphs. It was to these that I turned. I put a size 14 pheasant tail nymph on a leader of around three or four pounds in strength. I waited until the fish came close and just flicked the nymph a couple of feet in front of the shoal leaders. The impact was immediate. Two of the front-running fish darted towards the falling nymph and the first one there consumed it. It was a battle royal. Rudd fight alarmingly well, and when I eventually put my net under a fish that weighed two pounds ten ounces, I was simply aglow with excitement. Would I have pursued that rudd without advice from Mr. Crabtree? Probably not. That's another of my greatest angling moments that I have to thank the old boy for.

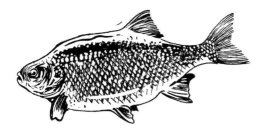

# Reels
# Fixed spool

Fixed spool reels are barely mentioned in Mr. Crabtree Goes Fishing. They feature briefly as the 'thread line reel' in the chapter on perch fishing but that's really as far as Mr. Crabtree goes with them. And for good reason. Fixed spool reels until the 1960s at least were crude affairs in the main. Their bail arms were clunky and even dangerous and their clutches notoriously unreliable.

From the 1960s and '70s, however, fixed spool reel technology moved forward in leaps and bounds. Today, their casting abilities have improved considerably but most important of all, modern day fixed spool reel clutches are entirely reliable. This means you can use them just as confidently with light lines as with heavy.

The advent of the bait runner option on most big fixed spool reels is also important. This allows the spool to run freely, especially when carp fishing and is a vital part of the self-hooking technique.

# Centrepins

You will notice in Mr. Crabtree that most techniques were based almost exclusively around the use of a centrepin reel. Today, centrepins have become redundant to a degree, replaced by the excellent, high-tech fixed spool reels of the modern age. However, centrepins still have two very important functions.

Firstly, it is my belief, and that of many others, that you cannot fish a river with a float successfully without a centrepin. It's true that fixed spool reels can do the job but they are clunky and comparatively inefficient. A centrepin is the ideal reel for virtually all river float work whether at close or at long range. It is well worth mastering the level of skill they demand.

Secondly, in my view a centrepin reel plays fish far more sensitively than a fixed spool reel. With a centrepin, you gain a direct connection to the fish without a fixed spool's gearing coming between you. This means that if you are fishing close and long casting is not a consideration, a centrepin is excellent for fishing slightly lighter lines than you could use with a fixed spool reel. I will often use a centrepin close in for carp and tench on stillwaters and barbel and chub on the river.

*Illustration by Bernard Venables from*
*Mr. Crabtree Goes Fishing.*

# Bream

"Then the Bream, the stately sailing bream...
what a tradition of fine summer sport is
associated with its name."

*Bernard Venables M.B.E. - Mr. Crabtree Goes Fishing.*

Fish care has changed dramatically, and very much for the better, over the past sixty years. When I was a Crabtree kid, the angling press would trumpet the massive bream catches of Bernard's day in grainy, black and white photographs. The keep nets would be spilled out, crammed with bream from Ireland, the Fens and, most especially, the Norfolk Broads. Bernard was one of the first to question this thoughtless treatment of fish and, today, we get our bream back into the water fast. Bream, like all fish, are delicate and vulnerable when out of the water and to corral huge numbers in keep nets did untold damage for very many years.

Bernard described the bream as 'stately' and that is exactly the right word. Admire your bream with its towering shoulders, its elegant fins, its great bellow-shaped flanks coloured deep yellow to gold to brown, mahogany and even charcoal black. River bream are especially fine: firm, muscular, slime-free and endlessly hard-fighting, wonderful fish.

WHILST STROLLING AROUND ONE OF HIS FAVOURITE LAKES ONE EVENING JOHN SPOTS A SLIGHT DISTURBANCE ON THE WATER...

HIS SUSPICIONS ARE CONFIRMED AS HE FOCUSES ON SEVERAL BREAM ROLLING ON THE SURFACE AS THEY MOVE ALONG A GRAVEL BAR ABOUT 30 YARDS FROM THE BANK...

BR1.

JOHN HASN'T SEEN THE BREAM IN THIS LAKE FOR A LONG TIME SO HE DECIDES TO PRE-BAIT THE AREA OVER THE NEXT COUPLE OF DAYS SO THAT HE CAN TAKE PETER FISHING FOR THEM WHEN THE WEEKEND ARRIVES.

TO GET A BED OF BAIT TO THE GRAVEL BAR HE CATAPULTS A MIXTURE OF GROUNDBAIT AND MINI BOILIES, THEN PHONES PETER TO TELL HIM HIS PLAN...

TWO DAYS LATER...

I KNOW YOU HAVE BEEN ITCHING TO FISH ALL DAY PETER... BUT BREAM TEND NOT TO FEED UNTIL THE LIGHT FADES...

AS THE BIG DAY ARRIVES PETER IS VERY EXCITED, YET JOHN DOESN'T TAKE HIM TO THE LAKE UNTIL THE LATE AFTERNOON...

Robert Olsen.

Like virtually every other species, bream, too, are larger now than sixty years ago when a seven or eight pounder was a fish of a lifetime. Tens are common now and twelves, thirteens or fourteens are around the triumphal weight on many waters. These super bream are often fish of the vast gravel pits but not always. My own biggest bream came from a Crabtree hole on a river and plenty of pits less than five acres have produced plenty of bream over fifteen pounds.

Of course, Mr. Crabtree taught Peter correctly. Bream feed best from sundown through the dark hours until sun up and a little beyond. Their eyes are notably large to utilise any light in the nocturnal waters around them and you will see them roll as the light fades and they mark out their territories. This is how I like to find bream if I can. Once I'm sure that the bream have settled and are going down to feed, I'll put out my ground bait, catapulted sparingly so as not to scare the fish from the swim. If you are sure of your location beforehand, spread a big carpet of bait in the late afternoon and you can hold a shoal of even big

fish until the small hours of the morning.

Everyone should spend some nights fishing for bream and my early, unforgettable experiences were at Gunton Lake, an estate water in North Norfolk. As a child, I used to hide in the darkening reed beds watching the bream become increasingly active as the colour went out of the sky. There were no electronic alarms for me in those days and I relied on cylinders of silver foil attached to the line between the reel and the butt ring. I can still remember the spooky rustling sound as the foil

was pulled again and again through the long grasses as the line trickled out in the wake of a taking bream. Later in my life, I can remember nights on the River Thurne, again in Norfolk, this time Broadland. A slight shift in the tide and a slight increase in the flow would bring the bream on, and when you netted them, you'd find them nestled on a bed of writhing shrimps. These fish were huge for me then, at four or perhaps five pounds. I remember they were so large I struggled to hold them, even in both hands.

The techniques for bream fishing have changed completely since the Crabtree years. Today, we have feeders, method feeders, quivertips, swing-tips, particle baits, exotic ground baits and a host of scaled-down carp methods that have all changed Crabtree techniques forever. They still don't have to be over-complex. A method feeder is straightforward, hugely effective and it is thrilling to watch the tip flick, quiver and pull round into another of these large, ponderous fish.

Like Mr. Crabtree and Peter, when it comes to bream fishing, I do live for the night. On stillwaters, I will always choose an evening between May and early October after a mild day, possibly with the lightest of westerly winds. It's good to get there early, to sit back, to watch the lake and wait for the sign of moving bream. Bream patrol routes are better recognised today than they were in Mr. Crabtree's day and we know that bream shoals follow well-trodden paths around any stillwaters. If you can get bait in before they arrive at their feeding grounds, you can be in for an electric night's fishing. It's not the fight of the bream that makes them so desirable. It is their elusiveness, their caution, the electricity they give out in the darkest of nights and, of course, their immense, mind-boggling size.

River bream mean a lot to me. There's a big, deep, almost still hole on the river close to me where the water rocks and eddies around twelve or fourteen feet, depending on the height. Here, in the gloomy recesses, at least a dozen bream live and have done now for decades. I know them and they know me and I fish for them occasionally, perhaps every year or two on a high summer evening as the dark seeps in. I'll generally fish a float, with an isotope, set two or three feet over depth. I will have done my baiting a couple of hours previously and spent a while in the pub waiting for the fish to find it. Like Mr. Crabtree, bread will be its base but today I'll probably season this with seeds and a scattering of corn. Sweetcorn and bream are rarely apart for long.

Bites are slow and deliberate. The float will cock, move across the idling current and disappear. The strike should be gentle but firm and far back, and the rod will hoop over to a fish that could well be over ten pounds. I'll never catch more than one. It's good to know the fish are still resident, still thriving after all these years. I caught my first fish from the hole back in 1974 and nearly forty years on, I feel such a strong connection with it that I would never want to exploit the relationship.

There's one similar type of hole – though perhaps not quite so deep - on the middle Hampshire Avon that I love equally. The water is perhaps seven feet deep and moves more quickly over a sparkling gravel bottom. You put the bait in, even in the brightness of an afternoon, and you'll watch the bream come from the dense weed beds around and begin to feed. A little red worm does the trick here, with perhaps one or two SSG shots nipped ten or twelve inches up the line. A quivertip is the tool. It will flicker and it will bounce but eventually it will pull round and it's the most marvellous thing to see one of the deeply-coloured bream twist this way and that in the glistening current.

There are those who don't rate bream. Mr. Crabtree, Peter and I aren't among them. The bream deserves our ultimate respect for the wonderful fish species it is.

# Floats

When Mr. Crabtree fished, float fishing was the most common form of the sport. Anglers of the middle 20th century were expert at float fishing both rivers and stillwaters. Today, sadly, most anglers probably fish the majority of their time with either leads or with swim feeders and miss out on what is, in my opinion, the most entertaining method of the sport.

If you're fishing stillwaters, you will probably be using a waggler float of one sort or another. If you're fishing on rivers, you will probably be using a stick float for close-in work and an Avon-style float if you are fishing further off.

These are just the basic designs and there are all manner of different styles out there. Perhaps the most important consideration is never to fish a float that is too light for the job. A heavier float, correctly shotted, is always easier to control and easier to cast.

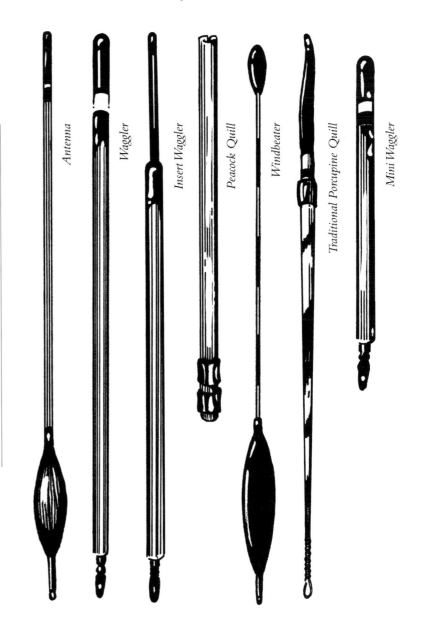

Antenna · Waggler · Insert Waggler · Peacock Quill · Windbeater · Traditional Porcupine Quill · Mini Waggler

*Selection of River Floats.*

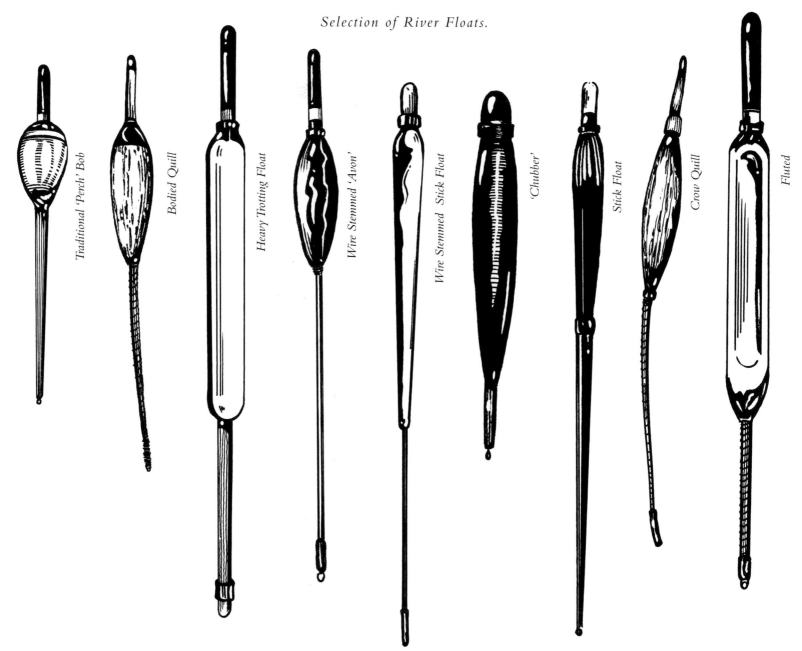

Traditional 'Perch' Bob

Bodied Quill

Heavy Trotting Float

Wire Stemmed 'Avon'

Wire Stemmed Stick Float

'Chubber'

Stick Float

Crow Quill

Fluted

*Illustration by Bernard Venables from*
*Mr. Crabtree Goes Fishing.*

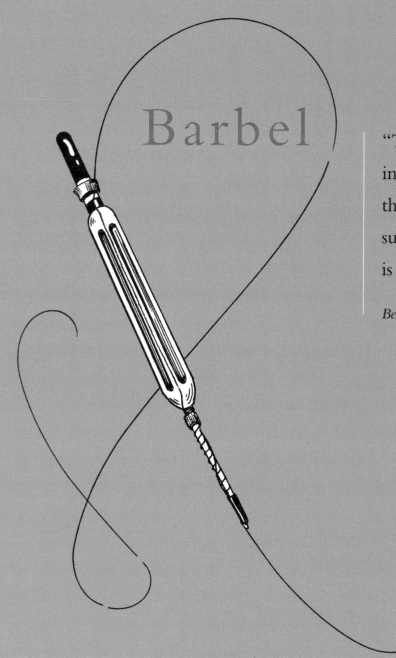

# Barbel

"The Barbel is a fish of the gravelly deeps. It lies in the clear chasms of water strongly scoured by the current. It is much sought in weir pools and such places and as might be expected from this, it is a strong fish that disputes hard for its liberty."

*Bernard Venables M.B.E. - Mr. Crabtree Goes Fishing.*

Looking back to my Mr. Crabtree-crazed childhood, it is the cartoon on page sixty-eight of the original book that most had me enthralled. It depicts the plunging float and the bullish, brutal power of the barbel as it bores away from Mr. Crabtree's rod. It is electric. You can feel the force of that fish surging off the page and, once it's netted, you melt to its gobsmacking, absolute perfection on the bank. Never, then, did I truly believe I'd ever catch a barbel myself but I did and they were even better in their reality than on that page conjured by Bernard, the master. I cannot praise the majesty of barbel more highly than that.

Over many years, I've come to know barbel and to adore them. If you are lucky enough to see them in a clear, relatively shallow river on a bright day, barbel are like no other fish. They're so compact, so strong, so in tune with the flows and currents as they sweep back and forth across the gravels. The colouration of each fish might well vary but it will always be sublime. The coral pink pectorals are almost a cliché but those

OVER HALF AN HOUR LATER...

HERE'S THE PLACE I WAS TELLING YOU ABOUT. A STEEP BANK WITH PLENTY OF TREE COVER AND A NICE EVEN PACE TO THE CURRENT THAT THE BARBEL ADORE.

I CAN'T WAIT TO GET STARTED.

THERE'S NO DOUBT THAT THERE ARE BARBEL TUCKED UP AGAINST THAT BUSH RIGHT NOW - BUT IT IS BEST TO TRY AND GET THEM FEEDING CONFIDENTLY BEFORE WE MAKE A CAST.

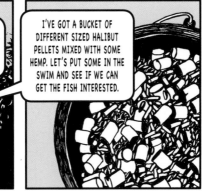

I'VE GOT A BUCKET OF DIFFERENT SIZED HALIBUT PELLETS MIXED WITH SOME HEMP. LET'S PUT SOME IN THE SWIM AND SEE IF WE CAN GET THE FISH INTERESTED.

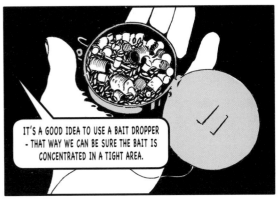

IT'S A GOOD IDEA TO USE A BAIT DROPPER - THAT WAY WE CAN BE SURE THE BAIT IS CONCENTRATED IN A TIGHT AREA.

WE LOAD IT WITH FREE OFFERINGS AND THEN LOWER IT TO THE BOTTOM WHERE IT OPENS AND THE BAIT WASHES OUT... 4 OR 5 GOES IS ENOUGH TO BEGIN WITH.

RIGHT PETER, WE'LL LEAVE THE BAIT TO WORK ITS MAGIC FOR AN HOUR OR SO AND I'LL KEEP POPPING BACK TO TRICKLE A LITTLE MORE IN AS THE DAY GOES BY, BUT LET'S TRY TO FIND SOMEWHERE WE CAN FISH CONFIDENTLY STRAIGHT AWAY.

flanks of golds, russets, browns and mahogany make barbel a magic species that will keep you hooked on fishing for life.

Bernard Venables, too, was captivated by the uniqueness of barbel. Bernard was at the tail end of a period of some magical angling and natural history writers. He was influenced strongly by Patrick R. Chalmers and you can sense Chalmers' own, greatest description of barbel in what Bernard himself drew and described. In 'At the Tail of the Weir' Chalmers wrote "But best of all I love the barbels because they roll like big brown and

white cats upon the golden shallows and sing in the moonlight with the jois de vivre of June. And because, so, they're all Thames to me and wild rose time and the streams running down from the weir." It's with this heart-stopping enchantment that Bernard cloaks Mr. Crabtree and sends him and Peter off to the barbel river.

However, even then, the barbel times were changing. Once again, remember that Bernard was writing in the post war days of rationing, limited finances and a general, nationwide

tightening of belts. Gone were those languid pre-war days when the rich barbel angler had his swim pre-baited with tens of thousands of lobworms before commencing to fish. Bernard also saw changes much more worrying. Mr. Crabtree is fishing during a period when it seemed that the best of barbel fishing days were almost done. There is a deep gloom about Bernard's vision when he writes "In the unseen channels through the weed lay many barbel and the loud sucking noises they made could be heard from far off. They were one of the many glories of this reach of the Kennet, a beautiful reach. Now all that is done. The bed has been dredged, the alternation of lovely shallows and deep, seductive pools has been swept away. The river has been canalized, the bends straightened. The matter dredged from the beds has been piled along the banks. The willows that lean so beautifully over the water have been cut down. The river has been 'improved.'"

Perhaps it is this sense of impending doom that makes Mr. Crabtree's barbel fishing so uniquely precious. Indeed,

Bernard was rightly wary of the future and, in the twenty-first century, abstraction on our rivers remains a major challenge to be solved. However, I believe that there is more good news than bad. When I first read Mr. Crabtree and first marvelled at his wonderful barbel, I was a child in the northwest and my local river was the Goyt, trailing out of Stockport towards the Mersey. I played along its banks as a boy, dreaming to see barbel in a river that ran every colour of the rainbow from the dyes pumped in by the textile factories along it. The place known as Otterspool was my haunt though otters almost certainly had not played there for at least a couple of centuries before. Today, though, barbel are returned to the Goyt and barbel can be caught at Otterspool. Had I have known that then, fifty years back, well, my skinny little legs would have buckled with excitement.

The deep dredging that Bernard rightly feared as the scourge of barbel rivers is, too, now largely a thing of the past. Barbel rivers are now treated more sensitively and the importance of preserving habitat is now widely understood. We have the Environment Agency largely to thank for that and, too, for stocking more and more rivers with small barbel to grow into big ones.

It is fair to say that barbel today are not only more widespread than in Crabtree's day but grow larger too. The record now stands at a shade over twenty pounds which Mr. Crabtree would never have dreamed of. It's worth remembering, though, that Richard Walker and his friends swore to seeing barbel of around that size in the middle Avon not long after Mr. Crabtree was written. Perhaps, we will never know about that and all we can say is that the barbel fisher has never had it so good.

Mr. Crabtree was a real Hampshire Avon man and for good reason. There's a bridge on the Longford Castle stretch of the middle Avon, just below Salisbury, where I have spent hours watching the beautifully formed fish of this crystal clear reach. Here, through the slats of the wooden floor you can watch the shoals of barbel sweep the gravel all day long. The fish are

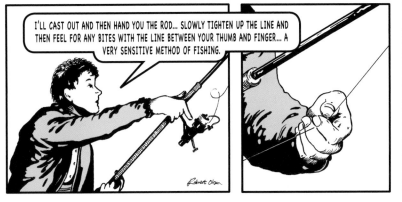

I'LL CAST OUT AND THEN HAND YOU THE ROD... SLOWLY TIGHTEN UP THE LINE AND THEN FEEL FOR ANY BITES WITH THE LINE BETWEEN YOUR THUMB AND FINGER... A VERY SENSITIVE METHOD OF FISHING.

A HOUR GOES BY BUT, DESPITE PETER MAKING SEVERAL RE-CASTS AND TRYING A LOBWORM AS BAIT NO BARBEL HAVE BEEN TEMPTED.

I THINK WE NEED TO TRY SOMETHING DIFFERENT PETER. THE WATER HAS CLEARED A LITTLE AND THE SUN IS WARMING EVERYTHING UP. GIVE IT ONE LAST CAST IF YOU LIKE AND THEN WE'LL WALK DOWN TO WHERE THERE IS SOME MORE OXYGENATED WATER AND TRY FLOAT FISHING BETWEEN THE FRONDS OF WEED. WITH THE SUN HIGH IN THE SKY THE BARBEL MIGHT BE SHELTERING THERE. HOPEFULLY WE CAN TEMPT THEM TO COME OUT AND TAKE A BAIT.

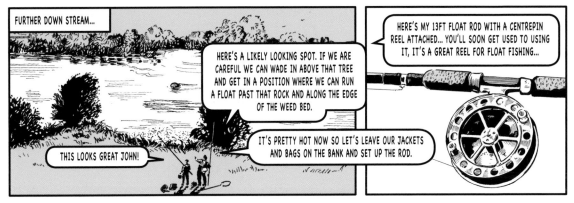

FURTHER DOWN STREAM...

HERE'S A LIKELY LOOKING SPOT. IF WE ARE CAREFUL WE CAN WADE IN ABOVE THAT TREE AND GET IN A POSITION WHERE WE CAN RUN A FLOAT PAST THAT ROCK AND ALONG THE EDGE OF THE WEED BED.

THIS LOOKS GREAT JOHN!

IT'S PRETTY HOT NOW SO LET'S LEAVE OUR JACKETS AND BAGS ON THE BANK AND SET UP THE ROD.

HERE'S MY 13FT FLOAT ROD WITH A CENTREPIN REEL ATTACHED... YOU'LL SOON GET USED TO USING IT, IT'S A GREAT REEL FOR FLOAT FISHING...

I'VE THREADED A BIG FLUTED FLOAT ONTO THE 6LB LINE AND ADDED THE BULK OF THE SHOT ABOUT 18 INCHES FROM THE HOOK. WE NEED TO GET THE BAIT DOWN TO THE FISH.

mesmerising, as graceful as in the cartoons and the hours pass in a wave of Crabtree magic.

Beautiful as the Hampshire Avon is, for me, though, the ultimate barbel river is a relatively recent one, the Wye. Barbel have been resident there little more than twenty years but they have made it their favourite home. Physically, the Wye is stunning, and that certainly befits the species but it is the never-ending variety of different water types that fires the imaginative barbel angler. The Wye challenges you to fish for barbel intuitively, using every last skerrick of your Crabtree skills. It doesn't matter how you want to fish for barbel, the Wye will provide exactly the right swim. Wye swims are just so perfect, so juicily appealing that it is easy to think they're a Crabtree cartoon, a fantasy and not a reality waiting to be fished.

If you can, get out the evening before you want to fish and pre-bait one of the deep, slow, mysterious pools that the Wye is famous for. I wouldn't go for anything fancy. A bucket of sweetcorn mixed with various size of pellets is about all you are

going to need. Throw in a dozen handfuls where you aim to fish the following dawn and try to work out roughly where the bait will come to rest. Then have an early night because the alarm clock is set for first light.

A perfect Wye dawn will be soft, still with traces of mist above the water. This is a time above all others when you will see the barbel roll in that majestic, unhurried way of theirs. Sometimes, a tail fin will hang like Excalibur above the surface of the Wye before disappearing with scarcely a ripple. Sometimes, you will see the shoulders of the fish and then just the eye itself, cautious, watching you in the pale light.

Fish simply. A rod, eight pound line, enough weight to hold bottom, a hook eight inches away and two grains of corn threaded on is all you will need. Swing the bait out, let it hit bottom, tighten up and point the tip towards where you think the bait is lying. Cradle the rod in your right arm so it is comfortable and then hold the line between the reel and the butt between the fingers of your left hand. Then you will sense the magic.

You will feel the barbel as they brush the line in their search for food. You will sometimes feel the lead being lifted and bumped a little downstream. Sometimes, your fingers will sense a very slow, gentle pull as the bait is actually being picked up and moved by the barbel's sensitive lips. Soon, though, there will come a quick jag, a heavy pull, a strike and the rasping scream of the reel. This is a glorious way to fish, so revel in the excitement and the directness. It's a way that people have fished for barbel forever and hopefully always will.

During the hours of daylight, it pays to be on the move and the Wye is such a big, under-fished river you can always find endless empty swims. If the day is hot, look for the barbel in the quick, oxygen-filled runs. Perhaps they'll be under bridges or under overhanging trees to escape the bright light. In the quick water, there's nothing to beat free-lining, the method we will use with chub fishing. Barbel will hammer two or three yards across the current to intercept two lobworms drifting their way over the gravel. Or, if you're feeling lazy, put on a swim feeder

AFTER AN EXCITING TUSSLE A SMALL BARBEL COMES TO HAND...

NICE FISH PETER - NO NEED FOR THE NET, JUST FLICK OUT THE HOOK WHILST SHE'S IN THE WATER.

JOHN HAS BEEN POPPING BACK TO THE BAITED SWIM EVERY COUPLE OF HOURS TO TRICKLE IN A LITTLE MORE BAIT AND PETER MANAGES TO CATCH TWO MORE SMALL BARBEL ON THE FLOAT. AS THE SPORT SLOWS THEY APPROACH AND GET READY TO MAKE THAT CRUCIAL FIRST CAST IN THE PRE-BAITED SWIM!

LET'S SEE IF WE CAN GET YOU ONE OF THE LARGER BARBEL THIS RIVER IS CAPABLE OF PRODUCING - WE NEED TO SNEAK UP ON THEM VERY QUIETLY - THEY LIE VERY CLOSE TO THE BANK AND ARE EASILY SPOOKED. I'LL HELP YOU DOWN, IT'S QUITE A STEEP BANK, WE NEED TO TAKE OUR TIME.

B10.

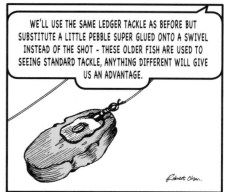

WE'LL USE THE SAME LEDGER TACKLE AS BEFORE BUT SUBSTITUTE A LITTLE PEBBLE SUPER GLUED ONTO A SWIVEL INSTEAD OF THE SHOT - THESE OLDER FISH ARE USED TO SEEING STANDARD TACKLE, ANYTHING DIFFERENT WILL GIVE US AN ADVANTAGE.

Robert Olsen.

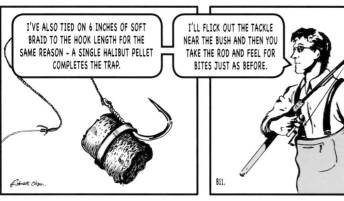

I'VE ALSO TIED ON 6 INCHES OF SOFT BRAID TO THE HOOK LENGTH FOR THE SAME REASON - A SINGLE HALIBUT PELLET COMPLETES THE TRAP.

I'LL FLICK OUT THE TACKLE NEAR THE BUSH AND THEN YOU TAKE THE ROD AND FEEL FOR BITES JUST AS BEFORE.

Robert Olsen.

B11.

EVEN THE SOUND OF THE SMALL STONE ENTERING THE WATER MAKES THE BARBEL SUSPICIOUS BUT, AS PETER HOLDS THE ROD AND WAITS QUIETLY, THE BARBEL SLOWLY RETURN AND BEGIN TO FEED ON THE LOOSE OFFERINGS THAT THE PRE-BAITING SUPPLIED...

THE FISH BEGIN TO SETTLE DOWN TO FEED AGAIN...

and flick it out into the very deepest pool. Again, you can touch leger or you can watch a quivertip if you're relaxing in the sunshine. The fishing won't be frantic at this time of the day but you will always pickup a barbel or two before the shadows being to lengthen.

Then, it's back to the hole that you've been baiting throughout the day. A handful of your corn and pellets every hour or so is enough to make sure that there are barbel sniffing around and waiting to be caught. And this is how I like to catch

them. It's simplicity itself. You will need a thirteen to fifteen foot float rod to give you more control and to let you anchor the float a rod length out. The delicate, forgiving nature of the float rod is part of the method, too. The float will generally be Avon-style, bulkier at the top to give good buoyancy. Remember to attach the float top and bottom and, as a general rule bulk the shot six to nine inches up from the hook. Then, set the rig up so you are fishing over depth approximately one and a half times deeper than the swim. In a four foot swim, fish at six foot, in a

...IT SEEMS LIKE AN ETERNITY BUT EVENTUALLY A BARBEL IS FOOLED BY THE SIMPLE PRESENTATION. AS IT FEELS THE BAIT WITH ITS BARBELS PETER FEELS A TREMBLE UP THE LINE THAT TELLS HIM TO GET READY...

I CAN FEEL SOMETHING JOHN... THE ROD TIP IS GOING!

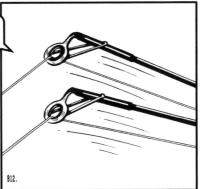

B12.

STRIKE PETER!

YES! WOW, I CAN'T STOP IT... IT'S NEARLY PULLING MY ARM OFF!

THE BARBEL IMMEDIATELY TURNS AND HEADS FOR THE MAIN CURRENT...

SHE'S STILL GOING... I CAN'T STOP HER.

Robert Olsen.

B13.

TAKE YOUR TIME... TRY TO KEEP THE ROD TIP UP PETER. I'LL GET DOWN BY THE WATER'S EDGE WITH THE NET.

THE FISH FIGHTS LONG AND HARD BEFORE PETER TURNS HER AND SHE BEGINS TO TIRE......

six foot swim, fish at nine foot and so on. You can reduce this in very slow water and you will have to increase it in quicker paced water, too.

Swing the bait out, let it settle and then tighten up so that the float is lying at around forty-five degrees on the surface, one to three yards downstream of the rod tip. Place the rod in a rest so that it is stable and watch the float carefully. Bites can be dramatic and come out of nowhere as the light begins to fade. Or the float can lie flat, move side to side or jab down a

fraction before it finally sails away. Keep your hand hovering on the rod butt so that you can strike fast, often as the rod tip is just beginning to pull round to the full fury of a hooked eight pound Wye barbel. You can lay-on with a float like this until the dark forces you off the river. It's now that the salmon will be most active, crashing out of the water as they begin to forge upstream towards their spawning beds.

To catch one or two barbel like this at the death of the day is more than enough. You've been up for fourteen or fifteen

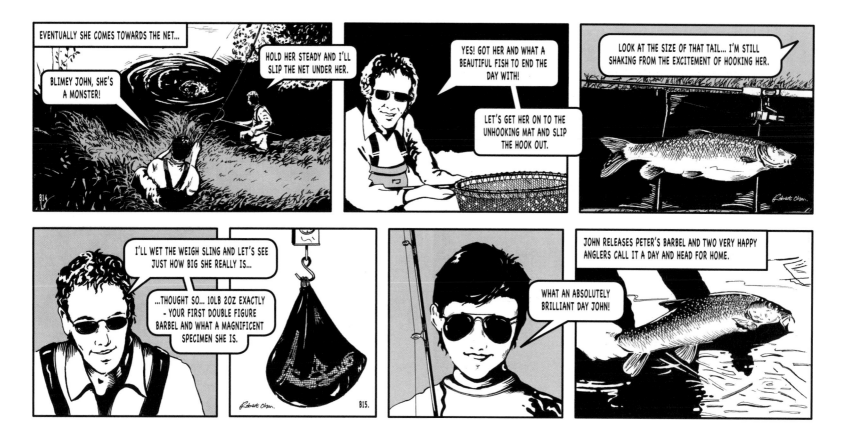

hours and you've taken seven fish in all, missed three bites and been smashed once by a fish that got behind a boulder and broke your line like cotton. You've used half a dozen cans of corn, a kilo or so of different-sized pellets, a feeder, two different floats, some SSG shots and three or four different-sized hooks. Everything has fitted neatly into a shoulder bag. Landing net, rod rest and apart from your rod and reel, that is all the gear you need for a perfect Crabtree day with the barbel.

It was on the middle Wye that my greatest ever Crabtree

barbel day took place. I was guiding a close friend, Geoff, on a wonderful beat of river below a scree of bright red sandstone cliffs. The water here is fast, strewn with rocks yet riddled with deep runs and pools. There is no road noise for the reach runs deep in a private estate. Peregrines have been known to nest high up on the cliffs and kingfishers dart endlessly up and down the rushing water.

Geoff wanted to fish total Crabtree. He had with him a 1950's cane rod and a centrepin from the same era. He wanted to use the float and trot maggots to where the barbel lay, flashing lazily in the sunlight like long, golden shields. We decided to fish intensively for two hours in the late afternoon as the sun left the water and give it everything we had got so we waded out across the shallows and positioned ourselves on the edge of the deeper, darker water and began to feed in the maggots in endless, squirming handfuls

Like Mr. Crabtree, I counselled caution. I asked Geoff to curb his bubbling, almost uncontainable enthusiasm and prepare the swim until the barbel were half demented by their gluttony for the grubs. Over thirty minutes we probably put in three, if not four pints before I allowed Geoff to make his first trot down the stream. Naturally, he was using a Crabtree-type float, well-bodied, heavily shotted and, inevitably, coloured red.

On the third cast, the float did not disappear as much as vanish. It seemed to javelin under the water and, almost without striking, Geoff's rod was hooped and his reel was singing.

Throughout the long, pulsating fight, the cane creaked and it groaned like a galleon's mast in a storm but, little by little, the fish came closer, its runs more tameable. I think Bernard would have enjoyed the sight of two men united in their excitement, in their love of barbel and their devotion to catching them in the right, float fishing way. We landed the barbel with a whoop of triumph and though, as we've said, weights are not important, the fact this fish weighed a few ounces over ten pounds was somehow significant. It was like every magical strand had been woven together into a day of complete barbel magic.

I have played football, tennis and cricket to reasonably high standards. I have climbed mountains both here and in the Himalayas. I have rafted white-water rivers. Yet, what I'd like this book to say to our children of today is that there is nothing, absolutely nothing, more exciting than a Crabtree day on the river.

# Watercraft
# Rivers

Rivers are immediately enticing. Look for the shallow, quick runs, often over gravel where, in bright, clear conditions you can sometimes see the fish feeding. Investigate the deeper, slower water adjacent. Look for deeper bends for bream, roach, chub and barbel. Learn to recognise 'creases' – those crinkly lines of water where the fast current divides from a slow eddy. These are favourite areas for chub and roach.

Try to be on your river both early and late for these are the best times to see roach and barbel roll on the surface.

*Illustration by Bernard Venables from*
*Mr. Crabtree Goes Fishing.*

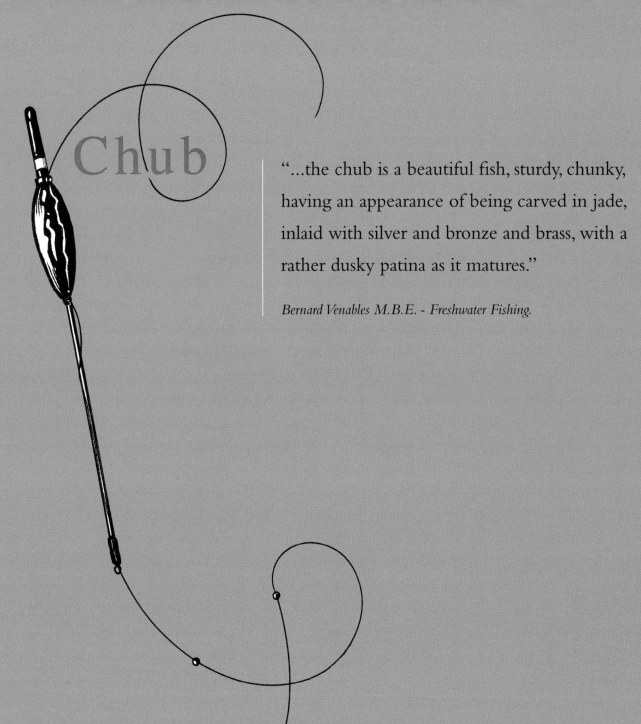

# Chub

"...the chub is a beautiful fish, sturdy, chunky, having an appearance of being carved in jade, inlaid with silver and bronze and brass, with a rather dusky patina as it matures."

*Bernard Venables M.B.E. - Freshwater Fishing.*

Mr. Crabtree knew his chub inside out. He realised a chub is as wary a fish as swims a river and that if you show yourself or make any mistake with presentation, you can kiss him goodbye. Just like the barbel, the chub has spread to many more rivers since Mr. Crabtree's day and my own beloved Wensum is a glowing example. There really are now chub available to us all, north, south, east or west, wherever we may live. The chub, like most other species, grows bigger today than back in the 1940s. When Mr. Crabtree caught a six pound three ounce Hampshire Avon fish, he considered it worthy of a glass case. Even if we still stuffed our fish today, you'd probably settle on a weight at least a pound heavier than that before making an investment with the taxidermist.

But you really don't need a chub preserved behind glass to keep alive the thrill of the species. See, or hook, a big chub in the clear river and your heart stops. There are monsters out there in our rivers that simply look the hugest of fish though we shouldn't really talk weights. Mr. Crabtree rightly thought that

MID-AFTERNOON ON A WARM AUTUMN DAY...

LET'S MAKE THE BEST OF THE WEATHER PETER AND SPEND A FEW HOURS TRYING TO STALK SOME CHUB - THERE ARE SOME REALLY NICE FISH IN THIS LITTLE RIVER BUT WE NEED TO FIND THEM FIRST.

I'VE BROUGHT ALONG A LIGHT CARP ROD AND A QUIVERTIP WHICH MAY COME IN USEFUL LATER ON.

WHERE DO YOU THINK THE CHUB WILL BE JOHN?

AFTER A 10 MINUTE WALK...

CHUB LOVE TO BE NEAR SOME FORM OF COVER AND THIS RUN USUALLY HOLDS A FISH OR TWO.

beauty is all and he was right. Still, the hope of a monster lurks in us all and now, in the new century, it really is chub monster time.

In all other respects apart from size and geographical spread, the catching of chub hasn't changed a jot. As Mr. Crabtree says, you can take them on just about any bait you care to imagine. Virtually any method will catch them, too, providing you have not spooked them with your presence or your presentation. I love chub because they bite in the sweltering summer heat or in the bone-crunching cold of deep winter. You can catch them in water crystal clear or dense as oxtail soup. They feed at night, dawn, daylong and dusk. You can catch them on the top, in mid-water and on the bottom. You will find them in the slacks and in the open water where the current is at its fastest. They simply offer every possibility to any angler's wildest imaginations. They are the fish of all seasons.

When I was a Crabtree kid, I learned of their ability to surprise. Then, much of my fishing was done on Sunday,

travelling on the charabanc, taking part in the club match. Old George who was partially deaf, would have slept from first whistle to last and always caught "not a sausage," when we came with the scales. One day, Alan, Geoff and I found him asleep, reeled in his tackle and impaled half a sausage on his hook. Two hours later, we found him awake, pacing with agitation, a three pound match-winning chub in his net. It still had the "bloomin' great sausage," dangling from its lips when it was landed. We sulked all the way home from the Trent as George babbled in the back about his success.

A Crabtree day out with chub is made perfect again because of its simplicity. Rod, reel, floats, shot, hooks, bait selection, net and you are off, free to roam the river wherever there are swims free and you still have the energy in your legs. There are scores of ways to catch a chub but perhaps Mr. Crabtree chose the best when he taught Peter how to use the float. Mash bread in a bucket with water until it's sloppy and dribble it into the head of a glide that is bordered by bushes,

reeds and overhanging trees. Feed in half a dozen handfuls to drift out close to the bankside features and then wait. Choose a float big enough for the river, probably an Avon or a Chubber, shot it mid-way to the hook and set it so the bread flake bait will drift a foot or so from the bed. Bites can come anywhere down the glide and the float simply buries. Strike with a firm sweep backwards and you will find the power of the freshly-hooked chub wildly exhilarating.

You can fish even more simply than this. Free-lining is exactly what its name suggests and you keep the line free of anything but the hook and the bait. To freeline substantially, you need something succulent and reasonably heavy. Two lobworms are excellent, or a dead fish, or a large, conker-sized chunk of luncheon meat. Choose a relatively quick piece of water, preferably four to six feet deep and running alongside the snags that chub so love. Let the current peel the line from between your fingers just slightly slower than the pace of the river itself. Keep tight to your bait so that you can feel it rise and fall with the flow. This is the poetry that exists in fishing and the pull of a taking chub is electric on your fingertips. Strike at once. The fish is on. This is magical.

Stalk your chub in the deep, dark water beneath the willows when the sun is high. Watch for their big, dark shapes passing through the shafts of sunlight. See those big, blunt heads and black-tinged tails and you know you've found a shoal of chub. Feed in your bait, flake, cheese paste, luncheon meat or pellets for half an hour until the fish are flashing,

digging, twisting, turning and competing for the food. Chub are competitive so profit from this and feed them up until they are in a frenzy and are unlikely to notice the glint of your line as it cuts through the bright water. When it comes to cast, you can use a quivertip which will lurch round when the fish takes. Or, more simply, hold the line between your fingers and point the rod at the bait. This is touch legering and you will feel the bite on your fingertips in just the same way as you did when you were free-lining. It's a heart-stopping moment. There will be a

WE'LL SLIP OFF THE FIXED SPOOL REEL AND REPLACE IT WITH A CENTREPIN - A FAR BETTER REEL FOR FLOAT FISHING A LITTLE RIVER LIKE THIS.

A LITTLE WIRE STEMMED AVON STYLE FLOAT, A No.8 HOOK AND A FEW SHOT TO COCK THE FLOAT ARE ALL WE NEED...

CB5.

HERE YOU ARE PETER, ABOUT TIME YOU CAUGHT US A CHUB - I'LL MASH UP A LITTLE STALE BREAD AS GROUNDBAIT.

THOSE CHUB HAVE DROPPED DOWN TO THE BOTTOM BUT THEY STILL MAY BE TEMPTED BY A PIECE OF BREAD FLAKE IF WE KEEP OUT OF SIGHT...

PETER CAREFULLY TROTS HIS BAIT DOWN THE RIVER...

AS IT NEARS THAT BUSH TRY HOLDING THE FLOAT BACK A LITTLE WITH YOUR FINGER ON THE EDGE OF THE CENTREPIN'S DRUM - THAT WAY THE FIRST THING THE FISH SEES IS THE BAIT!

CB6.

AS THE BAIT FLUTTERS DOWN A CHUB DRIFTS TO ONE SIDE AND SUCKS IT IN...

THERE PETER! YOUR FLOAT'S GOING... STRIKE!

jag on the line followed by a sure, slow pull as the fish turns and moves away confidently.

Mr. Crabtree taught Peter to take chub off the surface with a big, bushy dry fly and there is no more thrilling way to catch them when you can see them. A misty dawn is a fine time to surface fish but so, too, is a really hot day because chub do love the sun on their backs. Walk the river, looking for their big, bullish shapes holding position in the current. Once again, remember that black tail of theirs is a real giveaway. Try them with any amount of floating baits. Bread crust is hard to beat but so are dog biscuits, floating popper lures, plastic frogs or even bushy mouse patterns that are heavy enough to cast without a fly line. It's a glorious moment when the chub tilts, comes up towards your bait and its big lips part to reveal a flash of white mouth inside. Don't strike too fast. Wait for the bait to be engulfed, for the fish to turn and for the line to draw tight before easing into the fish. A chub taken from the surface is enraged: you'll never have another fight like it.

If you're wise, just as Mr. Crabtree advised, you will bait a swim little and often throughout the day and move into it as dusk begins to settle. The chances are as the dark seeps in, the owl is about and the wind hushes, the biggest chub of the entire, wonderful, exhausting day will be yours. Again, the fishing is simple. A quivertip, two SSGs on the line, depending on the current strength, a hook and a sample of the bait you've been feeding are all you need. Swing the bait in gently, let it settle, reel in the slack and point the quiver towards the stars. Sometimes an isotope attached will help you watch more easily and it looks a little like a satellite against the sky. Once again, there will be a knock as the chub picks up the bait and then the tip will go right round as the fish moves off. Now is the time to strike and to hold on hard. Make sure the clutch is wound down or the fish will get into the snags and your walk off the river will be a painful one. Get it right, though, and as the chub hits the meshes of the net, you will know you couldn't have had a better day doing anything else in the entire world.

That's what Mr. Crabtree taught us. Fishing is a challenge but it's fun, thrilling and exhausting. You experience the highs of success and the lows of disappointment. The adrenaline has never ceased to pump and your mind is a turmoil of emotions. You simply cannot wait to go chub fishing again. I know I can't. What I am waiting for is the approach of autumn, the turning of the leaves and the first frosts that clean the river to the transparency of glass. This is the true start of my chub wonder time.

Summer chub are fine but it's the autumn and the winter when they really fire the blood. That's when they are their dashing, biggest, most feisty selves. I have a stretch of river in my mind now, as I write, where the chub are perfect and where the fishing for them is all Crabtree. It's a small, upper river and it twists and it turns with delightful meanders over three miles of meadows and copse. Every bend, every pool, every glide will hold a chub or two and it's the sort of water you can explore throughout a short day to your heart's content.

The great thing about a day on a chub river like this is you can fish just every way Mr. Crabtree ever taught you to. You can trot. You can bounce baits. You can tether baits and watch the rod tip. There is nothing that is not possible but my best approach is this. I will walk all three miles and feed, approximately, thirty swims as I go, probably with a mixture of mash and cheese paste. When I have reached the bottom of the stretch, I'll stop for a while, possibly make a cup of coffee and munch on a sandwich and wait for the ground baiting to work its magic.

Then, with rod, reel, five pound line, hook and a single SSG shot, I will work my way back upriver, exploring every swim that I've baited.

Generally, I'll only have to wait a few minutes before I have my answer. Sometimes, a bite will be almost immediate and at others I'll have to wait a short while before the chub respond. And there will be other swims, too, where Mr. Chub is simply not at home. If I do fish all thirty swims, I'll expect bites from probably twenty and hope to land three quarters of those.

Missed chub bites are always part of the game. The chub, too, in this piece of river can be big ones. I'll hope for a handful of six pounders perhaps. I, personally, have never landed a seven, a legendary fish, but I know it's not that far away. Not that I'm bothered. It's the sport involved in such a day that really turns me on, not really the size of the fish. I'll have walked six miles at least. I'll have had endless action and excitement. I will have seen water voles, the barn owls, the passing kingfishers, roe deer in the thicket opposite, signs of a badger that's come down from the high sandy ground to patrol the riverbank after dark and all these things mean the world to me as an angler, as a disciple of the one and only Mr. Crabtree.

# Rods

In Mr. Crabtree's day, most anglers had a bare minimum of rods, which they pressed into service for all sorts of methods. In those days of austerity, there simply was not the money available to buy the armoury of rods most anglers take for granted today. In fact, most of my young life, I'd have one rod only and that would make do until it got broken, stolen or even lost.

Rods, too, were not the light, sensitive tools that they are today. I began with rods made of whole bamboo and only in teenage years progressed to the infinitely superior split bamboo models. Hollow glass rods were a great step forward and fibreglass rods dominated the scene in the later 1960s and early '70s. Carbon fibre began to appear in its earliest forms in the mid to late '70s and has now reached astonishing levels of sophistication. It's safe to assume that rod development will continue apace, and modern tackle shops have endless rod ranges to tempt you, but it is possible to simplify the choices you should make.

If I were to recommend the vital rods for today, I'd urge you to investigate an eleven foot, Avon-style rod that you can use for possibly eighty percent of your fishing. It will have a gentle through action, which means the rod bends progressively from the tip down to the butt. It will take lines happily between four and ten pounds in breaking strain and you can use it on stillwaters for light carping, tench, bream and even rudd and roach. On rivers, you will find it is ideal for chub and barbel. You can even use it as a light lure rod for pike and for perch.

A thirteen foot float rod is also a superb tool to have in your armoury. I feel that nowhere near enough people float fish these days and, if you're going to get the best of rivers particularly, float fishing is the way to do it.

Finally, I'd recommend a rod around twelve feet in length with a test curve of two or two and a quarter pounds. You will find this rod will do for the majority of carp fishing situations, especially when you don't have to cast over a hundred yards. This third rod will also double up in the winter as a dead bait rod for pike fishing.

There you are, three rods that in reality will take you through all the formative years of your fishing career.

*Selection of Rods.*

*11 Foot Avon-style Rod*

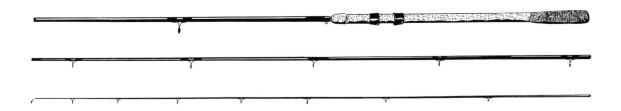

*13 Foot Float Rod*

*12 Foot Carp Rod*

*Selection of Weights*

# Weights & Feeders

Ledger weights have always played an important part in angling when there has been a need to get a bait down to the bottom and tether it there. Mr. Crabtree used several different types of leads, especially running leads, coffin leads and flat leads. Today, we have added considerably to this range with endless new designs. Carp leads, in particular, have taken lead technology to new levels.

What is entirely new since Mr. Crabtree's day is the swim feeder, a cage designed to be filled with bait, positioned on the line close to the hook. Swim feeders are fantastic tools, allowing you to put samples of your bait very close to your hook, even at long range. A closed swim feeder is perfect for packing with maggots. An open swim feeder can be plugged with ground bait and samples of the hook bait can be pressed within it. The method feeder is yet another advance. Ground bait is moulded around the feeder and the hook bait pressed into the mix. This is a superb method for carp, tench and bream in particular.

*Link Ledger*

*Flat Leads*  *Back Lead*  *Drilled Bullet*

*Selection of Feeders*

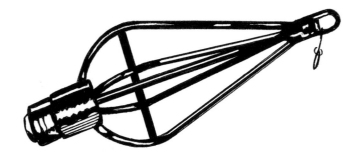

*Method Feeder*

*In-line Method Feeder*

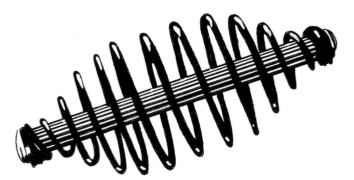

*Spiral Method Feeder*

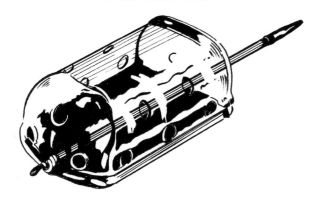

*In-line Maggot Feeder*

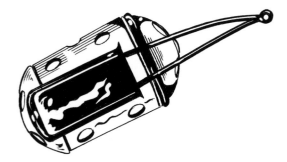

*Blockend Maggot Feeder*

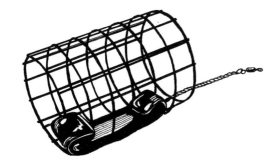

*Open-ended Cage Feeder*

# Baits Artificial

Any good tackle shop these days has a vast array of commercially produced baits. Shelves groan with boilies and pellets especially. These come in all manner of sizes, flavours and colours with endless different ingredients. Don't be afraid to keep things simple and ask the shopkeeper for his advice on what baits work well locally. There will also be a large choice of particle baits. For example, you will find flavoured and coloured sweetcorn, a traditional bait today but unknown in Mr. Crabtree's time. Also look out for hemp, seeds and endless selections of prepared nuts. You will also find a big choice of different ground baits, designed for different fishing situations and even different fish species. Try to keep your choices simple, once again with the advice of the tackle dealer. Make sure any baits that you have left over at the end of the session are safely stored, preferably in a vermin-proof bin. Never forget, too, that a trip to the local supermarket can pay dividends. Loaves of bread, cans of luncheon meat, meatballs and frankfurter sausages catch any fish that swims.

*Boilies*

*Hemp*

*Nuts*

*Luncheon Meat*

*Pellets*

*Mini Pellets*

# Natural

Mr. Crabtree fished a lot with 'gentles' as he called them. Today, we know these grubs as maggots and you can buy them in endless different colours. I would recommend red maggots for summer species like tench and carp, whereas you can't beat white maggots in the winter for roach and chub. For roach, in particular, maggots that have turned into their chrysalis form and are known as casters are especially effective.

Mr. Crabtree was rightly a great fan of the humble worm. Lobworms can prove deadly baits for barbel, chub, carp, tench and perch. Today, most tackle shops sell tubs of Dendrobaena worms that are also excellent for all the above species.

Keep your eyes open and use baits that you see around you. Slugs are traditionally excellent for chub and if you come across a dead frog, you will find that chub and perch will accept them readily. If you find any small dead fish in the margins, these can also prove excellent baits for perch, chub and barbel.

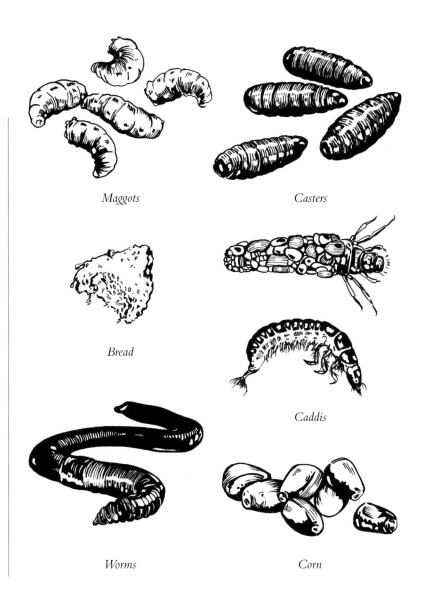

*Maggots*

*Casters*

*Bread*

*Caddis*

*Worms*

*Corn*

# Safety

When I was a Crabtree kid, I was allowed to go fishing on my own from the age of five or six, once I had learned to swim a length of the local pool and providing I did not talk to strangers, accept sweets from them, or get into their cars. Times have changed. Fifty years on, the rules on safety are far more complex.

Novices should always go out fishing under the care and supervision of an experienced adult, especially if the beginner is a child.

It's important to establish rules around the waterside. There should be no running or shouting, for example, and you should always look round before you cast to make sure it is safe to do so.

Young anglers should be encouraged to swim but also to wear personal flotation devices. These are essential if boat-fishing and strongly advisable even on the bank, especially when conditions are wet.

Polarised sunglasses are essential. Not only do they allow you to see into the water but they also protect eyes from flying flies, hooks or lures.

Clothing is vital. Make sure you build up the base layers and have a good, waterproof outer shell. You can always take layers off if the weather warms up but you can't put clothing on in cold weather if you don't have it with you. A spare set of completely dry clothing can be a lifesaver to have in reserve.

Make sure your footwear is up to the job. Wellingtons, thigh waders or chestwaders are always advisable but do ensure that the soles have a really good grip. My preference is for cleated rubber with iron studs attached.

A long-handled fishing net is vital so that beginners don't strain to reach a fish. This is also useful for removing rubbish from the water.

Take a First Aid kit to deal with any cuts, scrapes, bruises and bumps.

Take regular breaks for cold drinks in the summer and hot drinks in the winter. Drinking fluids prevents dehydration and heat strokes in the hottest weather.

Make sure that young anglers have plenty of sunscreen, wear hats and keep well covered. Make sure that the face, neck, ears and the back of hands are all plastered in sun cream. Try to avoid fishing in the middle of the day when the sun is at its height.

Bring plenty of insect repellent. Mosquitoes and midges are particularly unpleasant and anything with a Deet-based formula is likely to be effective.

Make sure you have the right equipment. Barbless hooks are kind on the fish but they're also kind on the young angler if a mishap occurs. Always make sure that forceps, pliers and disgorgers are at hand to make unhooking easy.

Don't let a young angler wade unless it's really important and, if you do, always obey the rules. Never let a young angler wade alone. Make sure any young angler wading wears his or her personal floatation device. Never wade in cloudy water because you need to know how deep you are going. Never wade in any current that is overly strong. Always check the bottom to make sure it's not slippery but covered in sand or gravel.

Be especially careful if you are fishing on piers, on slippery platforms, on treacherous rocks or on rain-soaked banks. It's always a good idea to have a young angler attached by a rope if the bank is particularly steep.

If the worst should happen and an angler should fall in, the first safety step is to reach out with an oar, tree branch, landing net handle or any other long object. If you can't reach the angler, throw them a lifesaving device. This can be a boat cushion or a buoyancy ring. Tie it to the end of a piece of rope so that you can pull the person to safety. If a ring isn't available, throw in anything that floats, even a beach ball can be used in an emergency. If a boat is available, then row to the angler in trouble and, ideally, take someone else with you to help pull the person out of the water. The angler should be pulled in over the stern of the boat with any motor completely shut off. Don't pull an angler over the side of a small boat as it can tip the boat over. Swim out to any person in trouble only as a last resort and only if you are an experienced lifeguard or have had lifesaving training. Never panic. Always keep a clear head.

Whatever your age, it is always essential to let people know exactly where you are fishing and precisely when you are due back home. Always ensure your mobile phone battery is well topped up and that important numbers are entered in it. If you are fishing into dusk, a good torch is absolutely essential and it's a good idea to have a back-up should the original fail.

Above all, never take risks. My own personal fear is steep banks when the river is high. If those banks are wet, especially, it's always a good idea to fix yourself with a rope in case of accidents. If possible, always fish with a friend in these situations.

Remember the old, but accurate, adage: Danger never goes on holiday!

# Knots

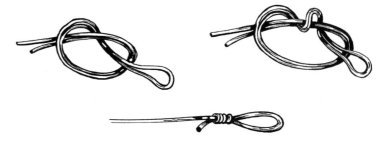

There are several fishing knot basics. Choose the right fishing knot and tie it correctly. Lubricate knots with water or saliva before drawing them tight. Draw knots as tight as possible and then trim the tag ends close to the knot itself.

Remember the best fishing knots are those that are reliable, easy to tie and that you have confidence in. My most used knot is an under-rated one, the half blood knot. I'd also advise you to learn the double overhand loop, the grinner knot and the knotless knot.

*Double Overhand Loop Knot*

*Grinner Knot*

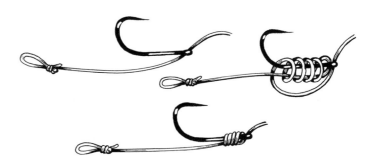

*Knotless Knot*

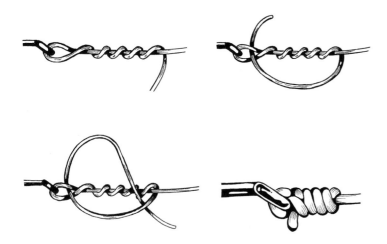

*Half Blood Knot*

*Sliding Stop Knot*

# Dos & Don'ts

**DO** make sure that you have an Environment Agency fishing licence if you are over the age of twelve.

**DO** ensure that you have permission to fish any piece of water.

**DO** check the weather report before going out to fish. Avoid particularly wet, windy or cold conditions.

**DO** try to join any local clubs. These will not only give you places to fish, but you will also meet other anglers and possibly meet up with accredited instructors.

**DO** make sure that mobile phones are well charged up. Do make sure that your family knows where you are fishing and when you expect to return.

**DO** keep fishing knives sharp but well-protected.

**DO** shut gates as a matter of course on farm lands and only light fires if these are completely safe.

**DO** always check out all fishery rules before commencing your fishing. Some fisheries have endless lists of complex rules so take the time to read and understand them all.

**DON'T** ever leave any litter. Take home with you any litter previously discarded around the swim.

**DON'T** put your fingers into the mouth of a fish. Even chub can be dangerous if your fingers get down to the throat teeth. Always DO use long-nosed pliers instead.

**DON'T** fish in areas where it is not permitted. Often, pieces of bankside have been declared off limits to protect wildlife, vegetation or for the angler's safety.

**DON'T** fish near to overhead electric power lines. Rods and poles containing carbon fibre conduct electricity so never approach closer than thirty yards at a minimum.

**DON'T** ever fish too close to any other angler and always ask permission if you are in doubt. This is especially important when carp fishing at extreme distances.

**DON'T** ever leave fishing line bankside as it is hugely dangerous to all forms of wildlife. Wire pike traces and treble hooks are just as dangerous, so always take these away safely.

**DON'T** ever go out in a boat unless you are completely confident, possess lifesaving devices and have friends on the bank that can help in an emergency.

# Thank you

This book has truly been a labour of love for all involved. We owe a debt of gratitude to Hannah for her wonderful foreword, to the Venables family for their friendship and support in entrusting us with Bernard's legacy and for sharing with us photographs from their private collection that give a unique glimpse into his life. Our thanks go also to Hugh Miles, Chris Yates, Kevin Clifford, Pat O'Reilly, Kevin Nash, Terry Hearn, Keith Arthur and Ali Hamidi for their contributions, which, between them, present a compelling argument for the breadth of Bernard's, and Mr. Crabtree's, influence. Finally to all of those 'on the inside' for their never-ending energy and determination to bring this book to publication. We got there.